FRYING TONIGHT

By the same author:
AMERICA THE CHANGING NATION
(Eyre & Spottiswoode, 1968)

GERALD PRIESTLAND

FRYING TONIGHT
THE SAGA OF FISH & CHIPS

'All lovers of fish and chips must feel a twinge
of regret that their favourite supper is
so often ridiculed on television, in plays
and of course in newspapers. It has been
going on for years and I think it is time
we in the Trade made a concerted effort
to quash this ill-founded humour.'

The Molly Codling Column
The Fish Friers Review
September 1971

GENTRY BOOKS · LONDON

Published by
Gentry Books Limited
55–61 Moorgate, London, EC2R 6BR
Layout, design and initial letters by Brian Roll
Set in 11pt Baskerville
Printed by Cox & Wyman Limited
London, Fakenham and Reading

Respectfully dedicated to
The Trade

Acknowledgments

The author wishes to record his gratitude to the many people in and around the fish frying trade who have helped him with this work. Prominent among them were:

Mr. Brian Ashurst of *The Fish Friers Review* and Mr. Graham Large of *The Fish Trades Gazette*, without whose vaults, shelves and files the book would have been totally impossible. Mr. Peter Worthington, General Secretary of the National Federation of Fish Friers; though I am sure he would wish me to state that I am not his mouthpiece and that neither he nor his Federation should be blamed for what appears in the pages following. The same must apply to Mr. Ray Ryall, Chief Information Officer of the White Fish Authority, and to his opposite number with the Potato Marketing Board, Mr. Edward Newman. Mr. Charles Rogers of the Shop Improvement Service of the W.F.A. is next on my list (indeed he *is* the Shop Improvement Service, single-handed). Mr. A. G. Williams of Associated Fisheries' Seafarer chain. Mr. Wilfred Bush lately of Harry Ramsden's Yorkshire Chip 'oile (and C. H. Wood, Bradford, Ltd. for the two photographs of Ramsden's). Mr. Zaki Nusseibeh of the Government of Abu Dhabi. Mr. Leonidas Onoufriou of Cyprus. A Mrs. Pang from Hong Kong. And among rangemakers Messrs. Triumph-Scarbron of Leeds, Messrs. Faulkner of Oldham and Messrs. Rouse of Oldham. Numerous unsuspecting friers, but before all to Mr. Maurice Williams of Truro and those three elder tribes of the Trade, the Lees family of Mossley, the Duce family of High Wycombe and the Malin family of Old Ford. And over all hovers the ineffable *Chatchip*.

On a less professional basis I am indebted to Maria Edmond for her delvings among the archives of the Fishmongers and the Wine and Food Society; to George Engle for literary serendipity; to Larry Hodgson for cloak and dagger work along the Costa del Sol; to Greville Havenhand for pioneer work in a chapter of his own book *A Nation of Shopkeepers* (Eyre & Spottiswoode); to my wife Sylvia for linocuts of fish and potato pottery; to my elder daughter Jennet for action photography

Acknowledgments

of Mr. F. Stratis' admirable Fish Bar at Bowes Park, London; to my sons Andreas and Oliver for hours spent brooding over trade journals in dusty basements; and to my family as a whole for their polite tolerance of this project which involved, for them, a somewhat monotonous diet.

In concluding this note I should warn of three things. First, that this is not a guide to the Fish & Chip Shops of Britain. Such a work, *A Gourmet's Guide to Fish and Chips* by Pierre Picton with D. J. Cooper, was published in 1966 by Four Square Books. Second, nor does this pretend to be a professional handbook on how to run your own fish shop. For such advice the novice should ask his friendly neighbourhood frier, or get in touch with the National Federation, the London and Home Counties Fish Caterers Association, Associated Fisheries, or the White Fish Authority (2/3 Cursitor Street, London EC4A 1NQ), which organize or can advise about training courses. Personally, I would not consider entering the Trade without family connections of some kind.

Third, the prices quoted in these pages do not necessarily apply today. A good frier never inflates his batter, but his prices are too often beyond his control.

G.P.

Contents

Illustrations

Many of the illustrations in this book are reproduced from original late nineteenth- and early twentieth-century blocks

Illustrations

Line drawings in the text

Illustrations

1. Salt and Vinegar

If you read no further, at least remember this: the moment the paper closes over its head, an order of Fish & Chips begins to die. That death is only made the more horrible by sprinkling it with vinegar. As for the traditional wrapping of old newspaper, progressive friers have fought against it for sixty years, and today, without a lining, it is actually illegal.

So when this book is burned in the streets of Leeds by howling hordes of West Riding purists, I shall face its martyrdom in good conscience. I have taken my stand. I have done my duty as I saw it. Wrapped-up Fish & Chips are an abomination.

Having said that, why go so far as to write a book about it? What is there to be said about Fish & Chips that could take so long?

Late in 1969 I returned to England after a long posting in the United States which had involved, among other things, the writing of a political-sociological book. It had been a strenuous undertaking, so that when my agent, John Parker, offered me Bryen Gentry's commission to write about Fish & Chips, I saw two immediate attractions: the research would help to reintegrate me with my homeland, and the subject offered a certain escape from the world of organized ill-will and violence which provides my everyday grist.

Both of these attractions have been realized. But a good deal more has come with them. My inquiries have not only refreshed my knowledge of Britain, they have also introduced me to corners of it I had never known before, particularly in the industrial North. For the fundamental truth is that Fish & Chips, like so much else in Britain, can only be understood in class terms. This is as true of Fish & Chips as it is of politics, dress, education or the theatre.

Karl Marx lived in London from 1849 to 1883, which takes in the very beginning of the first great Fish & Chips Boom, and it would have been a triumph of scholarship if I had been able to cite instances of his addiction to the dish and of his perception of its class significance. But I cannot. There is no proof that Marx *never* touched Fish & Chips, but the fact is he was personally bourgeois in his habits, and by the 1880s Fish & Chips were still anathema to respectable people. They were also largely a Northern custom, and could hardly have impressed themselves upon the founder of Communism as any more revolutionary than meat pies or jellied eels.

Much the same obstacles, only a little weakened by time, stood in my own way. How should a middle-middle-class Southerner, born in Hertfordshire and educated in Northamptonshire, Surrey and Oxford, appreciate that here was a road to the understanding of the proletarian infra-structure? There were only two occasions on which I cleared the barrier, but after each one I scrambled back on to what I knew to be my proper side of the fence.

Official Bag

During the Second World War I used to accompany my mother on shopping expeditions into the town of Berkhamsted. On our way home, pushing heavily laden bicycles up the Chilterns, we would pass a small Fish & Chip shop where we bought our lunch, to be consumed a mile or so further on among the concealing gorse bushes of Berkhamsted Common. The smell that oozed out of the shop was delicious, but it stood in a poor part of town near the chemical works, and it was quite clear to me that these picnics were exceptional, taken only because of wartime exigencies. When the war was over and there was petrol for the car once more, we never called at the shop again.

Later I went up to college at Oxford, and in the course of pursuing the girl who is now my wife, often took her to the Scala Cinema in Walton Street for a good cry over Jean Gabin, expiring on the Quai des Brumes and murmuring 'Embrasse-moi, vîtes!' Near the Scala there was a Fish & Chip shop, but it ceased frying in the middle of the big picture every evening, so that one was obliged to buy before entering the cinema and was then faced with a dilemma: whether to unwrap one's purchase in the stalls and eat it there and then in defiance of good manners and good taste; or leave it under the seat, plaintively growing colder and colder, to be eaten in digs two hours later? Neither course was satisfactory, and the dilemma only resolved itself when we left Oxford and went out hand in hand into the chipless middle-class world.

In *England Your England* George Orwell observes that besides being largely outside the European culture, England is the most class-ridden country under the sun, despite its capacity for emotional unity at times of crisis. Orwell also noted the curious cult of Northern snobbishness, based on the belief that only in the North was there real life, real work and real people. The Northerner, according to his own view, was grim, dour, plucky, warm-hearted and democratic; while the Southerner was snobbish, effeminate, parasitical and lazy.

Remembering that this is what people *think* rather than what is objectively true (if one could ever be objective about such qualities), these attitudes have proved remarkably tenacious of life since Orwell's day. Northerners still insist that only in their part of the kingdom is there real Fish & Chips (the Great Northern Chip is 'a real man's chip' I was told), and that only in the North are friers prepared to roll up their sleeves and sweat it out in the hellish discomfort in which God, or the Devil, intended chips to be fried.

Fish & Chips have provided me with a kind of archaeologist's cross-section of the vast, unexcavated mound of British working-class folk-culture; a limited and relatively shallow one, I admit, but nevertheless revealing. In September 1970 the school managers at Cudsworth, near Barnsley, found their pupils so accustomed to eating nothing but fish and chips, they did not know how to use a knife and fork to eat their school lunches.

For all the efforts of the White Fish Authority and the National

Federation of Fish Friers, Fish & Chips are still very widely regarded as wearing a cloth cap and wrapped in the *News of the World*. Quite affluent Northerners are still convinced that they are part of an essentially working-class way of life; while Southerners who are often no better off still regard them as 'not for us', as if they were some kind of charity relief for the poor. There are even sectarian and political overtones. Just as the North is thought of as being Chapel and Labour, while the South is Church and Conservative, so Fish & Chips are not in the Tory image. A watch on the queues outside the chip shops in Blackpool or Brighton at Party-Conference time will illustrate the truth of this. Business booms for the friers when Labour is in town and slumps when the Conservatives take over.

To outsiders this is all part of the half-lovable, half-maddening British obsession with traditions. If things go on this way, it should not be long before the chartered jumbo-jets of American tourists fly not to Bordeaux for the wine harvest, or to Munich for the Oktoberfest, but to Dagenham for the strike ritual, or to the last day of the Labour Conference for the singing of 'The Red Flag'. Fish & Chips are a part of all this, part of workers' rights, and when the British Army in Ulster wanted to raise the morale of its men it was natural to do so by launching 'Operation Codpiece'—an armoured mobile Fish & Chip van manned by one Corporal Williams from Warminster. In its way 'Codpiece' came close to the American image of Fish & Chips as something that Beefeaters with cockney accents serve out of thatched double-decker buses with fibreglass Tudor beams, chasing it down with crumpets and bottled Bass.

What is it about the very phrase 'Fish & Chips' that produces instantly at best a smile, at worst a smirk? It is only partly, I think, the nigger minstrel approach of the ruling classes making fun of their inferiors. There is nothing inherently humourous in the word 'fish', although there is something perky, cheeky and happy about the sound of 'chips'. Put together, they conjure up an atmosphere of warmth, cheerfulness, solidarity and contentment; and of being thoroughly British. The result is a kind of knee-jerk reaction upon which an editor or public relations man can rely when he is trying to season a dull page.

For years editors have been sending out reporters to see how many chips they can get for a shilling (an assignment, incidentally, which is no good for an undernourished expense-sheet). Recent examples are to be found in the *Evening Standard* of 26th February 1970 ('The Great Chip Scandal'), the *Daily Mail* of 20th July 1971 ('A 4p. one from the chips report') and the *Sunday Mirror* of 22nd August 1971 ('I've Had My Chips' by Harold Lewis). As the epigraph on my title page indicates, the Trade professes to be heartily fed up with such teasing.

The Fish Friers Review took particular exception to a survey published

It's shark and chips as fish tastes change

London Evening Standard, *24th January 1972*

in Southampton by the *Southern Evening Echo,* purporting to show that the quantity of chips was influenced by such variables as 'strength and vigour of the arm behind the scoop; sex of customer and/or server; the time when the chips are bought; and even the weather . . .' A prominent Newcastle frier retorted that while he personally tried to give four ounces of chips for 5p., he could not understand how some of his colleagues apparently managed to give nine or ten ounces. People didn't appreciate that a hundredweight sack of potatoes only made fifty pounds of chips, and that there were 'all kinds of complications'. Weighing out equal portions of chips all the time would hold up service; different shops had different standards to meet and different costs to cover; and, anyway, the customer was free to go elsewhere if he wasn't satisfied. This is typical of the ambiguous Love-Hate feelings of the frier towards his customer, and it may strike the layman that none of these replies was entirely frank or convincing; but at least it leaves the subject open till the next Silly Season which is, in fact, continuous. There is no 'close season' for Fish & Chips. Glance down the following mythical headlines, and you will agree that not one of them could fail to make its way in the popular Press, however trivial its significance:

FISH & CHIPS FOR PRINCE'S PICNIC
Two pieces of cod with chips, wrapped appropriately in *The Cornishman,* were served to Prince Charles, Duke of Cornwall as he visited Newlyn . . .

CHARLES IN CHIPS ROW
Leading fish friers complained today that wrapping Prince Charles's chips in newspaper had set their image back by fifty years . . .

BISHOP BLESSES FISH & CHIP SHOP
Recalling that Our Lord himself had not been averse to cooking and eating fish . . .

REDS BAN FISH AND CHIPS
Complaints by visiting Soviet diplomats of 'disturbing odours in our rooms' have closed down 87-year-old widow Doris Frier's . . .

R.A.F. IN FISH & CHIP DASH TO DYING MAN'S BEDSIDE
A dying man's request for 'one last nibble of good old Fish & Chips' brought an R.A.F. Comet jet hurtling . . .

100-YEAR-OLD DADDY SAYS 'FISH & CHIPS KEPT ME SEXY'
Holding his newly born son Aaron in his arms, Cambridge centenarian Moses Mogg thanked his daily packet of Fish & Chips for keeping him vigorous.

The game is endless. But there would be no point in playing it at all if Fish & Chips were not, in fact, a flourishing and cherished part of the national way of life—like keeping budgerigars or going to the seaside. The fact that foreigners may profess to like the dish, and even try to reproduce it in their own countries, does not affect our confidence that it is uniquely British and that no other people can really understand or imitate it. But that confidence is ill-founded.

There is an important ethnic aspect to Fish & Chips. Being at the bottom of the social ladder, frying has constantly been passed down to the latest and lowliest arrivals upon the scene. In the late nineteenth century, in the East End of London, there were many continental Jews in the Trade. Later, Italians took to it and there are colonies of English-speaking Italian friers in Newcastle, Glasgow, Edinburgh, Cardiff and Dublin to this day. The end of the Second World War brought in Cypriots, especially to London and Coventry. And more recently there have been invasions of Chinese and to a lesser extent Indo-Pakistani friers. I know of a Ceylon Tamil frier on the Finchley Road in North London, and a study of Yellow Page telephone directories will, appropriately, bring forth a treasury of Chinese friers. Bristol, which lists 126 shops in all, includes Chan Shiu Chung, the Mandarin Takeaway, four called Pang, Tsangs, Wong and Kam, and Y. L. Yip. Sheffield, with a huge list of about 270 establishments, has Fus and Chans, Li Tak On, Liu Oi Man, Liu Sing Che, Tsang Wan Choi and Ying Chung Lig among others. As with so many of our messier needs, we import foreigners to prepare our Good Old British Chips for us.

Fish & Chips would not be so lively a jest if they were less serious a business. They are, indeed, a great deal more serious than candy floss, winkles or roast chestnuts. They have beaten back the kipper challenge ('can't be eaten with the fingers and the smell lingers too long'), and they have a fair claim to being the original Takeaway Carry-out Convenience Fast-Food, almost a century ahead of the Hamburger, Hot Dog, Southern Fried Chicken and Pizza, all of which have now become very big business in the Age of Affluence and the Working Wife. The question is, whether the newcomers will crowd out and replace Fish & Chips, or whether Fish & Chips have some inimitable, irreplaceable value which will enable them to survive. I believe they have and that they will; though whether the same applies to the old-fashioned family frying business, I am less sure. The traditional frier is up against the might of the monopoly-capitalist Fish & Chip chains.

A remarkable thing about Fish & Chips is that the Trade can be read quite accurately as an indicator of consumer trends in the economy. Indeed, it is usually ahead of the Stock Market as a weather vane. Thus, as of March 1972, a consumer boom was clearly moving ahead, with approximately sixteen thousand Fish & Chip shops blazing the trail. Individually, they may have been small, but collectively this was no longer 'a petty trade'. Its sales totalled something like 130-million pounds a year, equal to the takings of all the French, Italian, Indian and Chinese restaurants in Britain, and surpassing the combined food sales of all the hotels and public houses. Both these latter groups sell dishes priced considerably higher than Fish & Chips, so the number of people patronizing the shops (75 per cent takeaways—25 per cent eating in the shop) must have been far greater than that of those eating in the pubs, hotels and foreign restaurants. However, the labour force in Fish & Chips—between fifty and sixty thousand people—would probably be considered lacking in productivity by a keen Organization and Methods man.

Besides being consumed, Fish & Chips are themselves consumers. The friers take 40 per cent of all the White Fish (that is, all fish except herring) sold in Britain, amounting to some five million hundredweights. They also use twelve million hundredweights of potatoes, which is about 10 per cent of the harvest. There is, in addition, the small matter of eighty thousand tons of oil and fat. Seen this way it is a banquet of surfeiting proportions, and the less we have to do with such statistics in future, the better.

As we shall see, the public has had its doubts from time to time about whether the Trade is quite as worthy as it considers itself. A survey carried out in 1970 uncovered suspicions that the business was 'no longer the British institution it had traditionally been' and that the product was no longer good value for money. But any defects are to be blamed on the frier rather than his wares; from the start, Fish & Chips have had a consistently good medical and nutritional Press. Put briefly, they contain between them a nice balance of proteins, carbohydrates, polyunsaturated fats (except where dripping is used), fluoride, calcium, iodine, nicotinic acid and vitamins A, B1, B2, C and D. It is not (as has been claimed) a complete diet in itself, but in a cold damp climate it is an ideal energy food for the heavy manual worker. Since potatoes are 80 per cent water it is a bit hard to condemn chips as fattening; and frying the potato rapidly preserves a great deal more of its vitamin goodness than boiling it.

Above all, Fish & Chips have endeared themselves to the British worker by their ability to linger comfortably in the stomach, reassuring him that he really has eaten and eaten well, for some considerable time after their consumption. There are few other foods, and certainly not Bamboo with Bean Sprouts, which have this ability to make one feel that one's lunch money has been well invested and not just sacrificed to the time of day.

The more one looks, the more aspects there are to our national dish. I have already mentioned the social, political, ethnic, nutritional and economic facets. I find, too, human, historical, literary, technical and mystical views to be had. From the human standpoint it is a story crowded with characters, from Mayhew's frier who preferred 'a gin-drinking neighbourhood' to ninety-eight-year-old George Mayston who has walked a mile-and-a-half for his Fish & Chips every day since he was ten. I see the friers' progress as the struggle of an untouchable sub-caste of British society to achieve respectability, a struggle against snobbery and bureaucracy which is still not entirely won.

Technically, meaning in the development of apparatus, it is a story of fine old British craftsmanship such as would have warmed the heart of Arkwright, Heath Robinson or Roland Emett, a craftsmanship which is alive and well and pounding away in lofted workshops in the North of England.

From the literary point of view, the surprise is that there is so little written about Fish & Chips, far less than there is about public houses or bee-keeping or cheese, so that one is driven back upon oral tradition most of the time.

But from the mystical point of view there is a wealth of meaning which lies beneath the surface giving rich, bass undertones to what at first appears to be no more than certain foodstuffs cooked in a certain

Rotary scrubber for sweated labour

way. Fish & Chips; Two in One and One in Two; not a takeover but a marriage, not a conquest but a companionship, 'the good companions' as Winston Churchill is reputed to have called them. Why is there no other comparable alliance? You might suggest Steak and Kidney, Strawberries and Cream, or Bacon and Eggs. But the first are too alike, the second too insubstantial and the third too *unsociable* to compete. Are there thousands of Bacon and Egg shops? A National Federation of Bacon and Egg Friers? Bacon and Egg jokes? There is simply no magic in them.

2. In the Beginning, Fish

First, catch your fish. He is a primal creature, a hunter's prey, closer to forest game than to farm beast. Science and the Bible agree in placing him first among sentient creatures: 'Let the waters bring forth abundantly the moving creature that hath life . . .' says Genesis. Even the Hindus put *Matsya-Avatara*, the Avatar of the Fish, first among the Incarnations of Vishnu. This feeling that the fish got here first, that he commands a medium we fear, that he has a moral ascendancy over us, can enter into our brain, is Good for us (especially, significantly, on Friday) gives us a strange respect for him. He has power over those who handle his body, and when he dies and rots, he can drag them down with him.

According to Fraser and *The Golden Bough* the ancient Syrians regarded the fish as too sacred to eat at all. The ancient Egyptians evidently did not share that view, causing the escaped Israelites to recall wistfully 'the fish, which we did eat in Egypt freely'. Homer indicates that the ancient Greeks did not care for fish, but later generations of Hellenes are said to have had a book of fish recipes by none other than Aristotle. The Romans relished fish and had officially controlled fish markets. One regulation, designed to hasten the clearance of supplies, forbade fishmongers to sit down at their stalls. The Arabs, being originally a desert people, took to fish as a result of settlement along the Persian Gulf and in Mesopotamia. The so-called 'Tigris Salmon' is one of the few things that makes life bearable in the deadly city of Baghdad. Brillat-Savarin, one of the few experts to regard fish as aphrodisiacal, attributed the proof to Saladin: who made the experiment of feeding two dervishes at first wholly upon meat—in which condition they remained immune to the temptations of a regiment of houris; and then upon nothing but fish—whereat they hurled themselves

Fish Incarnation of Vishnu: from Picard's Ceremonies *of 1741*

upon the temptresses with amazing stamina and skill. I have been unable to reconstruct this trial, for one reason and another.

The Incas of Peru (who also ate potatoes, and might conceivably be the ultimate ancestors of Fish & Chips) had their fish brought from the sea by relays of runners. To the north, the Kwakiutl Indians of British Columbia believe the salmon has an immortal soul (as did the ancient Gaels), and the Otawa of Canada believe in the transmigration of fish souls. The Hurons used to employ men to preach sermons to fish, urging them to come and be caught and promising that the Hurons would not imperil their spirits by burning their bones.

The Maoris of New Zealand put the first-caught fish back into the sea, so that it might pass good reports to its fellows. In Alaska the Tlingit install the first halibut of the season as a mighty chief, while the nearby Aino make a special hole at the back of their hut and furtively insert the first fish through it, so as not to scare away the others.

Halibut: a mighty chief to the Tlingit

In Christian cultures the fish has an advantage and a disadvantage. The disadvantage is that, unless bearing scales, it is proscribed by Holy Writ. Says Leviticus XI: 9: 'These shall yet eat of all that are in the waters: whatever hath fins and scales in the waters, in the seas and in the rivers, them shall ye eat . . .' Otherwise, 'they shall be an abomination to you.' The prohibition is underlined in Deuteronomy XIV: 9, for anyone who missed it the first time. What it means, for example, is that salmon, herring and carp are IN, while mackerel, lobster and scampi are definitely OUT (though for the not-over-orthodox, there are loopholes and modes of evasion).

Most Christians, however, have contrived to ignore all this, just as they have ignored the injunctions to make battlements on their roof-tops, avoid wearing garments of mixed fibre, forbid women to wear trousers, and stay away from church when 'wounded in the stones'—all of which are equally enjoined upon the Children of Israel by Deuteronomy.

Classifying fish by their fins and scales was a bit arbitrary in the first place, and a rapidly diminishing proportion of the early Church was brought up in Jewish homes. In any case, we have it from the New Testament that Our Lord Himself was a fish-eater. He spoke approvingly of the fisherman's calling, especially of Peter, and personally directed not only a miraculous draught but a miraculous mass fish-picnic, too. After His Resurrection, Christ consumed 'a piece of a broiled fish', and John XXI: 9 even implies that He engaged in charbroiling.

With this endorsement it is not surprising that the early Christians rapidly adopted the fish as their secret emblem. I was taught by my classics master that the letters of the Greek word Ichthus (fish) were taken as a code for 'Iesus CHristus THeou Uios Soteer',* which is neat but, I suspect, a later justification.

However it may be, fish was free to step into the gap left in the meat-less Friday; and here we approach a very special aspect of the fish question; for it is the only food I can think of which it has been positively compulsory for the British people to eat at any time. Under the circumstances it is small wonder that certain prejudices still linger, and a great wonder indeed that it should have become part of the National Dish at all.

Fasting is, in a double sense, a sacrifice. Taken to extremes it can induce ecstatic visions and mystical insights. The Church inherited it from Jewry, though the object of the *Friday* fast seems to have been to commemorate the day upon which Christ died. Once Christianity became a mass religion, it became increasingly hard to enforce total fasting; and so, from Jewry too, was borrowed the partial abstention from certain food, particularly meat. Fish is not meat, it is cold and bloodless; and so fish found its unique reserved market, only recently undermined so far as Catholics are concerned.

By the middle of the sixteenth century, after the breach with Rome and the Dissolution of the Monasteries, we find compulsory 'fysshe dayes', sometimes two a week, being enforced in England for purely secular reasons. On the one hand, the encouragement of the fisheries was expected to keep the shipbuilding industry in practice and the reserve of sailors well-stocked, in case they were needed for the maritime defence of the realm. On the other, farming was still primitive and the livestock population subject to decimation by disease and bad weather. Meatless days were a way of conserving, and even expanding, the cattle reserves. One day's abstinence a week would, it was claimed, spare 135,000 head of beef 'in a yeere in the Cittie of London'.

---

* *Jesus Christ Son of God, Saviour.*

Magistrates were still making returns of observance in the 1570s; seeing to the maintenance of the mediæval 'stews' or fishponds (some of them were still in use in the mid-eighteenth century), checking licences for exemption (26s. 8d. for a Lord, 13s. 4d. for a Knight, 6s. 8d. for persons of lesser degree), and administering punishment to defaulters. At one time the penalty was a fine of £3 or three months' 'close imprisonment'. At another we read of a London tavern hostess being pilloried for having meat on the premises during Lent; and of a wife of Hammersmith and a carpenter accomplice who, after trafficking in illicit pork, were ridden round the markets 'having eche of them a garland on theyr heades of the pygges pettie toes, and a pygge hanginge on eche of theyr brestes afore them'. But by the end of the sixteenth century, with two 'fysshe dayes' a week, enforcement became too sneaky and unpopular and the system collapsed. But the 'fish on Fridays' instinct lingered on, even through the Puritan Revolution.

Because of poor transport, the Englishman's fish, unless he lived on the coast, was almost entirely preserved or freshwater fish. But the Tudor age had seen the start of British cod-fishing off Newfoundland and the miraculous migration of the herring from the Baltic into the North Sea. It is pretty clear that the seas round Britain were crowded with fish well into the nineteenth century, though the shoals ebbed and flowed unaccountably, and the resources were grotesquely under-exploited.

According to W. H. Chaloner's essay in *Our Changing Fare* (Mac-Gibbon & Kee, 1966), the breakthrough came between 1780 and 1800. Growing demand from the population must have been one reason; more skilful fishing was another; but the most important was undoubtedly the improvement of transport, at first along the roads. In the year 1786, 500 horse-drawn vanloads of fish were sent to Billingsgate from Brixham alone. Turbot, plaice and salmon were in great demand, and there were complaints that the poor were as fussy as the rich.

The problem remained, though: how to keep the fish fresh. It was the Grimsby boats that pioneered the shipment of live fish in flooded chests, and at about the same time (the 1830s) the use of ice was spreading. It was harvested in blocks from specially flooded fields, and stored in underground wells or icehouses. Two such houses, for domestic use, have survived near Ashridge in Hertfordshire.

Mayhew (1861) found large quantities of both fresh and cured herring being consumed by the poor of London. 'The smell of herrings', he observed, 'savours from association so strongly of squalor and wretchedness, as to be often most oppressive.' Fish, we see, has begun its identification with the lower classes.

By this time the railways had arrived to put the entire trade on an industrial basis. Special 'fish trains' were being provided in the 1850s, and in 1852 Billingsgate was rebuilt to cope with the volume that poured in from all directions (including directly up the Thames). Similar developments were taking place in cities like Manchester, Birmingham and Liverpool.

By 1880, with refrigerated storage and artificially made ice freely available, and the steam trawlers vastly increasing the scale of landings, it occurred to the authorities that fish might play an officially sponsored role in nourishing the poor. The noted public nutritionist Dr. Mortimer Granville wrote: 'Fish might well and worthily supply the place of butchers meat as the staple food for the whole population. Pound for pound it is fully as nutritious . . . If the worried brain-working and nerve-straining population could be induced to substitute fish for the flesh of warm-blooded animals in its ordinary diet it would, I am convinced, be relieved from some of its worst sufferings and weaknesses, both mental and physical . . .' Dr. Granville might have added that, pound for pound, fish was often a good deal cheaper than meat, too. Might it actually prove to be the opiate of the masses? Why not experiment on those who were in no position to object?

A movement was accordingly launched under the banner 'Fish Dinners for the Poor'. Workhouse after workhouse, from Edmonton to Wrexham, from Nuneaton to Caister, and from Lambeth to Kidderminster, set down platters of steaming, economical cod before its inmates and waited for the reaction. Outrageously, a significant majority of those who were in no position to object, smelt a swindle and objected.

The Master of the workhouse at Wrexham told his Board of Guardians that 'The experiment of fish dinners for the inmates had been tried, and he had to report that the majority of them were decidedly in favour of beef. Some of them said that after eating a fish dinner, they felt hungry. But if the fish were continued, it would be a saving of Ten Shillings.' In spite of this, fish was dropped at Wrexham.

At Nuneaton 'Nine out of the forty-five inmates objected to the fish diet, whereupon it was suggested that in future a *white sauce* be supplied. The consideration of the subject was, however, adjourned.'

At Caister, too, in Norfolk, 'dissatisfaction among the inmates' was reported. Since the Guardians had only allowed the Master 2d. a pound for fish, while cod was 10d., this is scarcely surprising. The Guardians decided to switch to bacon—probably fat and streaky.

The Edmonton workhouse was a pioneer in the matter of Sauce for Paupers. The fish was served them with 'a little melted butter and anchovy', while yet saving a grand total of £3 15s. od. over the cost of meat. Apparently the sauce made all the difference, for no dissatisfaction whatever was reported from among the inmates, and one would have thought the savings alone were enough to please the stingiest of Guardians. But, no.

'Mr. Hutchinson asked by what authority the Master of the Work-house served melted butter and anchovy sauce to the paupers', and he belaboured the Master considerably for the extravagance. 'There ought to be some consideration for those who found the money to support these paupers. Many of the ratepayers could not afford anchovy sauce with their dinners . . .'

Then up rose Mr. Hobbs, to appease the sauceless ratepayers of Edmonton. He 'pointed out that spending two-and-sixpence on anchovy sauce while saving £3 15s. 0d. was hardly extravagance. Mr. Dodson offered to pay for the sauce himself. The Chairman said it was a real pleasure to see how the old people enjoyed their dinners. To see the pleasure and satisfaction that pervaded the countenances of these old people brought tears to his eyes. Was it worth while to quibble about this sum?' Cries of 'No! Shame! Never!'

But Reaction still had a sting in its tail. A Mr. Dart wanted to know why *Friday* had been selected as the day for the luxurious fish dinner?

Mr. Bennet: 'Because of the Roman Catholics who are there.'

Mr. Dart: 'Why not have it on Thursday? *We* do not study the Roman Catholics.'

The campaign to make fish loved among the poor staggered on for some years more. At the Great London Fisheries Exhibition of 1883 it is recorded that Mrs. Burdett-Coutts gave free meals of *Fish & Chips* to all the London poor who would attend; and in 1911 there was a curious exhibition in Manchester to stress the nutritional qualities of fish and *currants*. By that time, however, the propaganda was barely needed: the very cheapness of fish, its steadily improving quality, and that of the frying trade as well, were making converts voluntarily. But, as we shall see, there has remained in the back of many official minds a conviction that people *ought* to eat more fish and *would* eat more fish if only some way could be found of presenting it to them properly.

One difficulty has been to detach the fish from the reputation of its purveyors, which has tended to be rather uncouth. Thus in 1892 *The Fish Trades Gazette* felt obliged to editorialize as follows:

'Calumnies against their class have been so freely circulated that it behoves a journalist who has the honour to represent them in the Press to declare that for Probity, Shrewdness, Culture and Refinement the salesmen of Billingsgate Market . . . compare favourably with any representatives of Commercial England; and that in their relations with each other and outside their own circle, the merchants of Lower Thames Street are every bit as self-contained, polite and dignified as are the brokers of Mincing Lane or elsewhere.

'That it was not always thus cannot be denied . . .'

Which brings us to the present day.

Official bag

This book keeps trotting off inquisitively down odoriferous side-alleys, and will continue to do so; but it does not intend to go far down that occupied by the fish-*catching* industry. However, it is here that the most significant changes affecting our central theme have taken place—technically, economically and politically.

On the technical side I will say only that, unless you are that mythical old-timer who used to get his shelf-haddock 'straight off the boat that caught it offshore', your average shop-fish today is of incomparably

32

The Great British Invention.

'I claim this lunch for Queen Elizabeth!' (White Fish Authority poster)

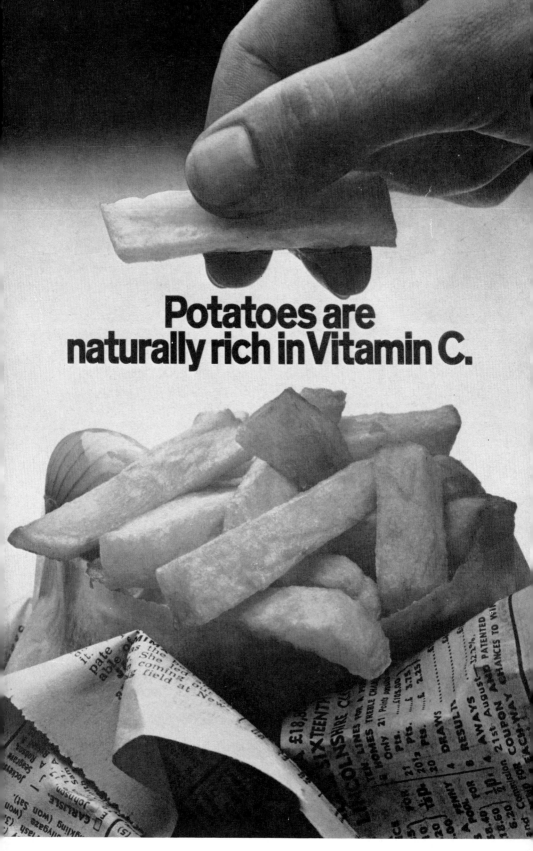

Potato Board poster: friers resented the newsprint image

better quality today than it was thirty, forty or fifty years ago. Well over half Britain's fish is now caught as far away as Iceland, Greenland, Bear Island and Newfoundland. The freshest landed is already a week old, and that is the longest that mere chilling in ice can keep fish anything like 'fresh'. But fish that is quick-frozen on board within a few hours of being caught, frozen to below 18 degrees centigrade, will taste as good as that and better for a matter of months.

Economically, the brute problem is over-competition, coupled with the mysterious migration of certain species away from British waters. To quote Mr. Peter Worthington of the National Federation of Fish Friers: 'The plain fact is that there is not enough fish to go round . . . 40 per cent of all the fish caught in the world now goes into international trade . . . Fish is an international commodity, sought by many nations. The position has been reached where there is competition for supplies between *countries*, whereas until recently the main factor affecting prices was the competition between individual users . . . The price structure here is very much influenced by the price which the highest bidder—the United States of America—can afford to pay.'

That is one example of world fish politics. Others are to be found in disputes like those which Britain has had with Iceland and with the European Economic Community, and which the United States has had with Latin America, about how far a fishing country can fence off the waters along its coasts for its own private use.

What it all adds up to, as far as Britain is concerned, is steadily rising prices and declining landings of fish. As I write, fish prices in general have tripled over a period of three years. Fish that cost 2s 11d. a stone in 1914 is £3.50p. a stone today, though there is not a great deal of sense in trying to work that out as a percentage increase.

With the possibility of pricing itself off the market altogether, the fish trade has tried to take hold of its destiny by calling in Public Relations. Inevitably, the first thing was to conduct a survey, and the survey showed 'an alarming lack of enthusiasm for and interest in fish among housewives. The main users were the older people—either from the upper-middle class or from the bottom of the social scale. The strongest regions were the North of England and Scotland. Conversely it was the younger housewives, from the middle of the social scale, and most frequently living in the Midlands and South, among whom fish was at its weakest.' (My quotation is from a speech by Mr. R. F. Ryall, Chief Information Officer for the White Fish Authority, dated October 1970.)

The trouble was, apparently, that fish had a pretty dreary image all round. They were irksome to prepare, pallid in appearance, lacking in virility, wanting in goodness compared with meat, a poor buy and generally out of date in an age of tinned soup and T.V. dinners.

C

33

The White Fish Authority raised a levy of three-quarters of one Old Penny per stone of fish sold by wholesalers, and equipped itself with a publicity budget of £400,000 a year. (The wholesalers were unhappy about this and made trouble, arguing that only the retailers stood to benefit from the campaign.) There were posters in Fish & Chip shops, adverts in the papers, commercials on the Telly and in the cinemas. Indeed, Fish & Chip commercials actually won medals at Venice and New York.

White Fish Authority prose poem

Good and nourishing.

Fish & Chips are packed with vital body-building protein. Natural vitamins, too. It's a good, hearty meal the whole family enjoys.

A meal in itself.

Serve up Fish & Chips as they come – nothing simpler. Or, like some mums do, you can have a vegetable ready on the stove to go with them.

The most immediate impact was felt by Fish & Chip shops near cinemas, which is logical enough. A further nauseating survey, this time of the things schoolchildren left on their lunch plates, taught the W.F.A. that Fish & Chips and fish fingers were among the most popular lunches served in school; so part of the campaign was directed at local education authorities. Fish, they were told, was 'more cost-effective'. 'It is vitally important to the fishing industry that school children develop a liking for fish', pleaded the W.F.A., '*Unfavourable experiences with fish at school may well result in indifference to, or even absolute rejection of, the commodity for the rest of their lives.*'* It was a sobering thought, if a somewhat Freudian one.

Not only had the image of fish to be repainted; people had to be con-

* *The italics are mine—with relish. G.P.*

vinced that with the prices of almost *all* foodstuffs rising astronomically, fish was actually a somewhat better buy than meat. 'Ounce for ounce,' concluded the W.F.A., citing a quiverful of the latest papers and reports, but echoing the essence of what Dr. Granville had proclaimed ninety years earlier, 'white fish contains more protein than any meat except chicken meat . . . There is not much to choose between fish and meat for vitamins, except that herring is a rich source of vitamin D.' Purist fish-friers would probably have preferred the Authority to omit the remark about chicken.

Visually the campaign stressed the bright, fun, trouble-free image of patriotic Fish & Chips. There was not much that could be done for the fast-declining wet fish trade, apparently bound to move increasingly into the deep-freeze cabinets and speciality counters of the super-markets; except to assert the virility of fish in general—the one food that still calls forth Man the Hunter, that involves danger in the catching, and that can rely upon the nation's pride in its seafaring sons. Over a hot, red tableau of trawlermen heaving in agony on their nets, the W.F.A. intoned the following prose poem:

> Fish is wild and pure.
>   We don't *grow* fish.
>   We capture it,
>
> leaping and flashing,
>   lean and alive.
> Fresh from the cold,
>   clean sea.
>
> Fish is not fattened
>   for market
>
> Fish is the only food men
>   still go out and hunt.

To my mind a masterpiece of overtone cultivation and insinuendo. A slightly less spectacular poem, printed below a tempestuous seascape (the work, I understand, of a genuine fish-merchant), declared:

> Our fishermen are hunters
>   They work with cunning
>   and with courage,
> To capture the leanest, cleanest
>   food that Nature provides.

Pure, lean, fresh, clean—unique Fish Qualities being implanted in the consumer's mind. But did they take root?

Well, it's true that *post*, and quite possibly *propter*, the campaign, 10 per cent more housewives confessed to feeling some pleasure in preparing fish (*'Just a tiny tingle when I chopped its head off, maybe'*); that 'fewer housewives now would feel hesitant about offering fish to relative strangers' (*'Go on, have a haddock!' 'But we've scarcely been introduced . . .'*); and that, according to the pollsters, 'the heavy stress on the functional, dull characteristics of fish has begun to break down,' (*'If you bring that dreary old cod in here once again, I shall scream!' 'But Mum, he's such fun and ever so nice-looking . . .'*).

But what in fact took root in the public mind, more than anything else, was the steadily rising price of a food that so many had regarded as marginal anyway. A survey taken in the autumn of 1971, after sixteen months of the W.F.A. campaign, showed that while 65 per cent of the housewives interviewed served fish 'because it is very nourishing' and 45 per cent 'because it is full of natural goodness' (a checklist distinction which escapes me), only 18 per cent ticked the answer 'because it is cheap to buy'. The W.F.A. thinks it sees 'a more positive image of fish' emerging, and I, for one, will drink to that. But the Authority can also see that the higher prices go, the less often the housewife serves fish. Since its campaign began the proportion of those vital, up-and-coming

Prices rise as fish landings decrease

Fish Friers Review, April 1972

	1970		1971	
	Tons	£s	Tons	£s
Cod	298,900	27,684,000	253,000	33,560,000
Haddock	41,670	4,660,000	36,940	4,740,000
Plaice	38,000	5,486,000	38,800	6,304,000
Dogfish	5,446	390,000	6,715	530,000
Coley	31,415	1,345,000	35,910	2,103,000
Total (Gt. Britain) ..	719,000	63,830,000	704,000	78,733,000

younger housewives serving it once a week or more has fallen from 56 to 49 per cent. Older housewives are apparently set in their fishier ways, notwithstanding the 24 per cent increase. This is not to say that things wouldn't have been worse without the advertising; only that fish in modern Britain is stuck with this image as a marginal, optional food.

So is it doomed to extinction? Total extinction in the zoological sense, I doubt. Despite the trend of British landings, and the cries of 'Overfishing!', *world* catches continue to rise, and there are varieties of fish in the Pacific, Indian and Arctic Oceans we have yet to sink our teeth into. I cannot believe that International Conservation and the farming of sea fish will remain in the background much longer. That fish, in the sense of a sweet haddock kit, will move into the luxury class is much more likely; but meat eaters may do no better. The processed extruded fishchip or the anonymous plankton finger on the one hand, the battery-raised chicken, rabbit or guinea-pig on the other, will probably be the housewife's lot. And whether Fish with Chips can remain a working class staple much longer, I seriously doubt.

3. Dark-skinn'd Andean Root

ext, dig your potato. There is a striking contrast here between present image and past history. Chime the word 'potato' and you get a dull thud; such overtones as there are are drab, fat and earthy; Irish without being romantic, agricultural without being pastoral. Who would have thought that the potato's background was really exotic, erotic and magical? Also choked with confusion and mistaken identity.

Let us define this for a start: we are talking about, or trying to talk about, *Solanum tuberosum*, a plant low-foliaged, insignificantly flowered and endowed with edible, starchy roots, belonging to the family *Solanaceae*. This includes not only such appetising specimens as the eggplant, garden pepper and tomato, but also such undesirable members as the deadly nightshade, thornapple, henbane and tobacco. The whole pack of them are most at home in the Americas, and it is there that we must look for our starting point.

To be perfectly honest, where we actually look is in Roze's old-time classic *L'Histoire de la Pomme de Terre* (1898), or, better still, in Redcliffe N. Salaman's stupefying monograph *The History and Social Influence of the Potato* (1949). Dr. Salaman, one-time Director of the Cambridge Potato Virus Research Station, devoted more than forty years of his life to this banal and unresponsive vegetable, and one can only stand before his work, head bowed, in deep respect. He chose no easy row to hoe.

There is no doubt at all that the potato (or potatoes) were brought to Europe from the Americas by Spanish explorers and *conquistadores*. Columbus, who landed in Haiti in 1492, found the natives of the Caribbean eating the *batata*, which sounds familiar but was *not*, in fact, our potato. The *batata* was a sweet potato or yam (correctly, a sweet potato of the *Convolvulaceae* family; yams are *Dioscoreaceae*, and much good may

39

Sprouting spud

it do them. The point is, neither are *Solanaceae*). Colombus took some *batatas* home, where they were served crystallized, like *marrons glacés*. They were not a horticultural success in European climates, but their very scarcity and exotic origin aided the reputation, pressed upon them as upon so many other newcomers in that age of faulty nutrition and sexual frustration, as an aphrodisiac. And it is this 'potato' that leads us astray when we pursue the word into the Shakespeare concordance.

The Merry Wives of Windsor, Act V Scene 5, finds Sir John Falstaffe at his randiest. His lady is almost in his grasp and welcomes him ambiguously as "My deer!". Lecherously, Sir John answers: 'My doe with the black scut! Let the sky rain potatoes; let it thunder to the tune of Greensleeves, hail kissing-comfits and snow eringoes:* let there come a tempest of provocation, I will shelter me here. (*Embracing her.*)'

The 'potato' must thus have been generally acknowledged as appropriate to Sir John's typhoon of lust; and we meet it again in another bawdy episode, in *Troilus and Cressida*, Act V Scene 2. Thersites ('a deformed and scurrilous Greek') is playing the voyeur on the lovers. He exclaims: 'How the Devil Luxury with his fat rump and potato-finger tickles these together! Fry, lechery, fry!'

It would be pleasant to be able to claim this as the earliest known reference to chips, but I am afraid the meaning is a good deal coarser cut. To have a potato-finger was like having a sweet tooth, for lechery. The strange thing is that the sweet potato's (the *batata's*) reputation as a love-food survived as long as it did, into Napoleonic Paris.

With such a forerunner, there was bound to be confusion when later waves of Spanish explorers came across the true or *Solanum* potato. This they seem to have done in Peru (though Soviet science insists on Chile) during Pizarro's conquest of 1531–5. The evidence of Peru's curious potato-shaped pottery suggests that the Incas and their predecessors had been cultivating the root for some two thousand years. Maize does not do well on the Peruvian highlands, and some other staple had to be found. Consequently the life-giving potato came to be invested with the same magical-religious significance that we find investing the personification of corn in Central America and Mexico. The fact that the

* *Candied Sea Holly (*Eryngium*)—a noted aphrodisiac, now discredited, like everything else.*

root could be propagated by hacking off pieces containing 'eyes' and burying them in the ground gave rise to a mythology in which the god-hero was mutilated and dismembered by his enemies, only to rise again wherever his limbs had fallen. Some of the potato pots appear to illustrate this with chopped-off features.

The sowing of the potato by the Incas was sometimes accompanied by blood sacrifice. In earlier times it probably involved the slaying of children, but in 1547 the Spaniards observed a ceremony in which a year-old llama was killed and its blood sprinkled over the seed potatoes. These had been escorted to the fields in a procession of gorgeously dressed boys and girls, with farmers carrying the implements of cultivation. On another occasion, following a fight in which several Indians were killed, the womenfolk rushed in to collect the blood and scatter it on the fields where potatoes were to be grown. This has been compared with the practice, in parts of Ireland, of sprinkling the fields with holy water and of starting to plant seed on Good Friday.

Inca potato-effigy pots

The earnest Dr. Salaman was told by a fellow potato-scholar of a particularly ludicrous folk custom still surviving in Peru, under which, if a woman were to unearth a more than usually grotesque-looking potato, she would run with it to the nearest man (who was obliged to stand his ground) and strike him hard in the face with it. It is the kind of folk custom which the average Peruvian folk male must feel might well be allowed to die out.

By the 1560s there was still no mention of *either* 'potato' in European botanical writings. Clearly it was not yet growing in Europe. Even if the Spaniards had brought themselves to think of the Andean variety as a food appropriate for themselves, shipping it back to Europe from the western seaboard of South America would have been difficult. A friar named Hieronymous Carden is reputed to have accomplished it about the year 1570, and we read of a new type of edible root from America being consumed medicinally in Spain in 1573, and being purchased for a monastery hospital three years later. It was certainly being *grown* in

Europe by 1590, because soon afterwards it begins to appear in North European 'herbals', or catalogues of useful plants.

The Inca name for the Andean potato was *papas* or *papa*, which must have embarrassed the Spanish, to whom the name meant 'father' or even 'Pope'. John Gerard's 'Catalogue' of 1596 names *Papus orbiculatus*, nicknamed in a later edition 'The Bastard Potato'. Gerard writes of 'knobbie rootes . . . some round as a ball, some ovall or egge fashion'. He makes it clear that, to him, the sweet potato is the true or common potato; but he claims to have received *Papus orbiculatus* from Virginia (where the first English settlement attempts had been disastrously unsuccessful) and that it had grown and prospered in his own garden, the fruit maturing in September. It had, he said, the 'pleasant taste and vertues' of the earlier *batata*.

Salaman thinks Gerard cannot have been talking of the potato we mean today, because the solanum potato was not native to Virginia and had not yet been transplanted there. Gerard must have got hold of some kind of ground-nut, perhaps the Algonquin *Openauk* root, or even the Jerusalem Artichoke (sometimes known as *pomme de terre*) which we know came to England from the gardens of the North American Indians, and which was growing here during the early years of the seventeenth

John Hawkins: potato importer?

century. To make matters worse, when the solanum potato got to Italy, it was called *tartuffi* or *tartufoli* because of its resemblance to the truffle, and migrated across much of Europe under variations of the German form *Kartoffel*.

But how did the true potato get to England? John Hawkins brought something back from Venezuela in 1565, but they were probably sweet *batatas*. Sir Francis Drake acquired local *papas* for his stores on the coast of Chile in 1578; but it is guesswork whether he brought any home. There is a legend that he did and that he gave some to Raleigh, who grew them on his estate at Youghal in Ireland, but threw them out after mistakenly eating the berries instead of the roots. The only people who seem to have accepted Drake wholeheartedly as the European sponsor of the potato was the population of Offenburg Baden, in Germany, who erected a statue to him in the nineteenth century, hailing him as 'Introducer of the Potato into Europe in the year of our Lord 1580'. The statue, showing Sir Francis with a potato flower in his hand and a frieze of tubers round the plinth, might have illustrated this chapter today, had it not been removed and melted down by the Nazis.

All we can be certain of is that Ireland was the first corner of the British Isles to grow potatoes in quantity, that they cannot have been sweet potatoes and that they cannot have come from Virginia. The old, last-resort theory of flotsam from the Armada is, I suppose, possible but unlikely.

Meanwhile the scholars were still trying to sort things out on paper. It was the Bauhin brothers of France who introduced the botanical name *Solanum*, and shortly after, in 1601, the Dutch botanist Clusius traced the origin of the species to Quito, Ecuador—which at least disentangled it from the Caribbean and Virginia. In Italy, he reported, potatoes were being boiled with mutton like turnips or carrots, or else fed to pigs. But like most scholars of the day, Clusius could not resist popping in a bit of juicy hearsay as if it were fact, adding: 'They are flatulent, *and therefore some use them for exciting Venus.*'

Why flatulence should have been considered a concomitant of randiness (in my experience Venus is repelled and put to flight by it), I fail to see. The legend seems to have been transferred hopefully from the old *batata*, and it spread like wildfire. In 1619 there are reports of potatoes being baked in their jackets in Basel, where 'they eat them for exciting Venus and increasing semen'. Dr. Tobias Venner of Bath, in his *Via Recta* of 1620, finds them 'somewhat windy and inciting to Venus'. And by the year 1710, William Salmon has them down in his *Herbal* as 'Moderately Diuretick, Stomatick, Chlisick, Analeptick and Spermatogenetick. They nourish the whole body, restore in consumptions and provoke Lust'. And to make it all perfectly clear he adds: 'They increase the Seed and provoke Lust, causing fruitfulness in both sexes ... Good against Impotency in Men and Barenness in Women ...' Elsewhere, Salmon has much the same to say about carrots; and it may well have been that almost any addition of natural vitamins to the unbalanced diet of that age would have made people feel fitter, in bed or out of it. It is, however, a line of publicity which the Potato Marketing Board might wish to exploit today, with the judicious use of 'morning after' photographs, along the lines of a recent series advocating vodka.

But being new and foreign and *not mentioned in the Bible*, potatoes were equally liable to be blamed for anything that went wrong. Early in their European career they were banned in Burgundy for causing leprosy, and on into the mid-eighteenth century they were denounced from time to time for setting off outbreaks of pox, scrofula and 'fever'. Diderot's first Encyclopædia dismisses them as 'insipid and starchy . . . One blames, and with reason, the potato for its windiness,' he says. But there is no room for Venus in the Age of Reason. In a later edition, though, the Encyclopædia commends the potato as a weapon against famine, and points out that the diseases for which it has been blamed are notably rare among the fecund Irish, already the world's record potato-eaters. (Today the record is held by the Paraguayans, with an average consumption of a quarter of a ton per head per year.)

Inca potato pot: note eyes

The Spaniards had been the first to recognize the root's merits as cheap slave-fodder. In Europe, as we have seen, pigs and invalids got generous helpings. But efforts to fob it off on the poor as an economical filler met with mutinous resistance. Everybody knew that fresh fruit and vegetables caused fevers and bloody fluxes, and were in no way a substitute for good honest beef, beer and bread. 'No Potatoes, No Popery' proclaimed one eighteenth-century Sussex demonstration, just as a later Chartist banner demanded 'More Pigs, Fewer Parsons'. In Ireland, however, sheer need broke down prejudice. Cultivation of the potato was beyond the experimental stage by 1633, and by 1697 we read that the Irish were 'mighty lovers of Potatoes—an earth apple'. They were also notoriously bad farmers, and the 'dig a hole and stuff it in' technique was precisely on their level. Impressed by the results, Charles II's Royal Society recommended that potatoes be planted throughout the kingdom as an insurance against famine. This view was a century ahead of the Encyclopædists, and it is interesting that France, fatherland of gastronomy, lagged so far behind the rest of Europe in recognition, use and development of the potato. Conservative and insular as ever. Not until 1771 did Antoine Parmentier manage to get his improved varieties on the Parisian menu, winning the belated recognition of Louis XVI. If only Marie Antoinette had thought to respond: 'Let them eat *pommes de terre!*'

Even so, it took the American and Napoleonic Wars, with the threat of isolation from foreign grain supplies, to force the British farmer, under the prodding of the newly formed Board of Agriculture, to take the crop seriously. Essex, Lincolnshire and Kent were among the first counties to take it up on a large scale, working partly on Irish advice and experience.

Among the treasured archives of my family is an agricultural note-book kept, about the mid-1840s, by an obscure retired sea-captain named William Scrymgour. Scrymgour was an insatiable self-educator, and his pages upon the treatment of potato disease are not only in-triguing in themselves, they also help to explain why so little could be done to resist the potato blight that struck and ravaged Ireland at that time.

After mentioning experiments with soap-residue, soda and muriatic acid (hydrochloric acid to us), he goes on: 'The potato disease is the result of *sexual debility* resulting from the *uninterrupted double-sexual propagation of the potato*. Note the beneficial effects of crossing with other plants: 1. *Helianthus tuberosus*—2. *Dalia variabilis*—3. *Cyclamen europeum*—4. the *Carduus hispanica* not of the bulbous genus. With which the potatoes are cut into eyes and placed in the earth close to the genus of plant with which they are to combine . . . The result of each combination was not only without disease in the potato but the root was improved in size, beauty and flavour; the latter partaking of that of the plant with which it had combined, the combination with the cyclamen being most pro-ductive, these plants having transferred their vigour to the potato.' It sounds almost mediæval; but if an educated mariner-farmer could believe it, what hope was there for the development of more effective treatment that might have saved Ireland?

Eating between seven and fourteen pounds of potatoes each per day, dependent on them almost exclusively for health, growth and energy, the Irish population spurted ahead in a wild recovery from its Crom-wellian depths. The increase between 1780 and 1840 has been reckoned at about 170 per cent. It cannot have been due to the Industrial Revolu-tion or improved medical care, for neither reached Ireland. Law and order, low expectations, early marriage, peat for fuel and the potato to eat; together these set off the Irish population explosion. '*Vive la pomme de terre!*' cried one observer, venturing the judgment that the Irishman's diet was probably healthier than that of the English labourer. Neverthe-less, the Irishman was putting his head in a potato noose.

Between 1728 and 1851 there were no fewer than twenty-four major crop failures. Prior to 1845, the harvests of 1839, 1841 and 1844 had been general or widespread failures. In 1845, with a population of nine million relying upon two million acres of potatoes, a new kind of blight or 'murrain' arrived, ironically from North America, by way of the Isle of Wight. Overnight it could reduce a field to a blackened, rotting wasteland, and the tubers underground to a stinking pulp. Treatment with copper sulphate or Bordeaux Mixture was undreamed of.

The Blight struck again in 1846 and 1847; deaths must have totalled more than a million, and combined with the emigration that followed, halved the population of Ireland. The horrors of the Famine, and the callous indifference towards them of most Englishmen, are beyond description. Perhaps one can only bring them home today by naming Biafra or East Bengal as comparable: bloated bellies, stick limbs, the eating of earth and even of corpses—it was all there, across the channel from callous England.

According to Cecil Woodham-Smith's tragic history *The Great Hunger* (which relates about as much as one can bear to read about the Famine), the potato was then on its way towards becoming as much a staple for the English as it was for the Irish. We must be thankful that the Famine at least helped to prevent us going too far down that road. With the Repeal of the Corn Laws, the spread of the railways, the growth of an industrial consumer economy and a worldwide network of trading partners, the British people embarked upon a thoroughly mixed diet which has, despite many other defects, made us one of the world's healthier races.

Two World Wars brought the potato strongly back into its own, stimulated by the blockade of grain and other food imports. In 1914, British farms were producing little more than three million tons of potatoes. By 1918 that had been raised to almost five-and-a-half million. Another boost during the Second World War, employing a

Potato: but does flatulence excite Venus?

more advanced science of farming, and the level reached was eight-and-three-quarter million tons by 1945. (It is now in the neighbourhood of six million.)

Who of my generation has forgotten the officially sponsored, potato-bloated recipes of that folksy tipster 'Potato Pete', the straw-chewing cartoon yokel? Or, within less than two years of Pete's retirement, the sudden *volte face* that had us queueing for potatoes 'on the ration', and the papers full of advice about how good it was for us to eat *less* potatoes? Small wonder the British public remains, as it has always been, profoundly sceptical of propaganda directed towards its dinner plate.

As to the cooking of the potato, I have cited evidence that from the earliest times it was baked or boiled (the Peruvians made beer of it, too; and there is vodka or schnapps). E. Smith's *Compleat Housewife* (*c.* 1729) recommends boiling potatoes in their jackets, then peeling them and serving them with butter. But, as an alternative, they could be peeled, *sliced* and fried in butter. There is, however, a crucial distinction between *slicing* and *chipping*.

The American Hannah Widdifield (Philadelphia 1856) gives two recipes for fried potatoes, both of which require pre-boiling. Georgina Hill's sixpenny *How To Cook and Dress Potatoes in one hundred different ways* (1866) gives a recipe for *Pommes de Terre Frites* which calls for 'thin slices quarterwise' and other 'pretty ornamental shapes'. But it is not until *Kettner's Book of the Table* (1877) that we find the issue frankly faced: 'In English kitchens the fried potatoes are very uncertain because they are cut in too thin slices; also because they are done in a flat frying-pan with a sparing supply of butter or dripping. Instead of cutting the potatoes, like the English, into shillings, French cooks cut them into square plugs, about the length and thickness of the little finger . . .' And away we go into the whole business of deep, boiling fat and a wire basket and the need to turn the heat up when the chips are plunged in. But I have reason to believe that what took so long to reach the lady housewife was already commonplace among the caterers to the poor.

Today, thank goodness, the annual cycle of the potato involves none of the political, ecological or commercial drama that has closed in upon our fish. Although some imports are needed to bridge the gap between crops (a gap which can cause as much alarm among fish friers as the Bay of Biscay), by and large Britain grows enough potatoes for herself, and sometimes more than enough. In 1971, the carefully controlled acreage yielded 10 per cent more than expected and almost swamped the market. The Potato Marketing Board (sister in many respects to the White Fish Authority) had to undertake price-support buying on a massive scale, and launched a potato publicity campaign very similar to the 1970 Fish Bang. Posters, recipes, exhibitions (including a working model 'Potato Fayre' built by the inmates of a Scottish prison), sponsored cookery books and 350,000 booklets on how to *Slim with Potatoes*— nothing was spared.

But the enemy this time was not price, but the image of fatness, and the increasing reluctance of the housewife to slosh about in muddy water peeling the brutes. (Incidentally, anyone over thirty must have mused occasionally over the following miracle: not so long ago it was considered compulsory to buy a pound of mud from the greengrocer with every stone of potatoes. 'This is Nature's Way,' we were told, 'and if they are washed, they will go rotten.' Nature has suffered another setback, and it is no longer so. What worries me is, who buys the mud now?)

More and more, the potato is coming out of the field and straight into the factory. Twelve per cent of the British crop is processed in one way or another, the largest proportion emerging bagged as potato crisps (confusingly called 'chips' by the Americans), garnished now with exotic flavours ranging from bacon, roast beef and onion to 'smoked venison' and 'chuck waggon'—whatever that may be. There follow dehydrated mashed potato, tinned potatoes (handy for popping into tinned stews), and blanched, frozen, chilled and par-fried chips, in twenty-pound lots ready for the Fish & Chip Trade. Chilled, the chips will last up to six days; frozen, considerably longer. One firm claims to have launched a special $\frac{9}{16}$ inch thick *frier's* chip, one eighth of an inch thicker than the usual caterers size, and designed to give customers the more homely feeling they expect from a Fish & Chip shop.

It is, alas, but a short step to the bulk-dehydrated potato which is then re-hydrated and extruded through a square tube to be cut up into completely uniform chips. It will almost certainly come, and who will bother then with the arguments about whether King Edwards should have been displaced by Majestics, or whether the newer Pentland Crowns and Desirées are better than both? Nobody will listen to the Scots, calling for Redskins and Dr. McIntoshes (which, to the palates of some chip connoisseurs, are the finest of all). As Dr. Magnus Pyke, of Glenochil Food Research Station has observed, the potato is one of the most inconvenient of foods, and science is bringing it to heel. There seems only one, last refuge for the few remaining potato addicts: to insist on it baked in its jacket (and not wrapped in aluminium foil, at that).

Potato Marketing Board poster: our tuber, right or wrong

ounder of the Trade? Little Joe with drunken John Lees (note clogs and jam butty)

Lees' of Mossley: little change in seventy years

VARIETY	DESCRIPTION OF TUBER
First earlies	
Arran Pilot	Kidney; skin white; on exposure, blue-purple develops fairly rapidly around the eyes, while the remaining surface may become mottled; flesh white; eyes shallow.
Home Guard	Oval; skin white; on exposure, faint colour may develop at the eyes; eyes shallow; flesh white.
Epicure	Round, irregular; skin white, but turning pink on exposure; eyes deep, ridged; flesh white.
Ulster Prince	Long kidney, sometimes hooked at heel end; skin white; on exposure, blue-purple rapidly develops; flesh white; eyes shallow.
Second early	
Craigs Royal	Oval, slightly flat; eyes shallow; flesh white to pale lemon.
Maincrop	
Majestic	Kidney (pear-shaped to long oval); skin white; on exposure, pale red-purple usually develops at the eyes; eyes shallow; flesh white.
King Edward VII	Kidney (oval to pear-shaped); skin white, more or less splashed with pink; characteristically smooth on surface eyes shallow; flesh white.
Redskin	Round; skin pink; flesh white to pale lemon; eyes shallow.
Kerr's Pink	Round (somewhat flat); pink, dented at heel; eyes usually medium, sometimes deep; flesh white.
Dr. McIntosh	Long-oval to kidney; skin white; on exposure, the tuber greens rapidly and develops a faint red-purple colour at the eyes, this spreading slightly over the surface eyes shallow and mainly on the point; flesh white.
Pentland Crown	Oval; skin pale yellow; on exposure, tuber turns mainly green; eyes shallow at the rose end, being set in a shallow depression; flesh creamy white.
Pentland Dell	Long oval (tend to be banana-shaped); skin smooth pale yellow; on exposure, slowly turns red-purple about eyes; shallow eyes at the point of the tuber; flesh creamy white.
Record	Round to oblong, slightly flat; skin white with yellow tinge on exposure, blue-purple develops at the rose end; eyes shallow to medium; flesh yellow.
Golden Wonder	Kidney (pear-shaped); skin russet; eyes shallow, saucer-shaped; flesh white to lemon colour.

Fish Friers Review, May 1972

4. Sources—An Interlude

or an outsider to research a book about the fish frying trade is like being an infidel in an Arab mosque: you can go through all the motions, but you'll never be one of the boys. Part of the trouble is, friers have always been men of the *pan* rather than the *pen*. They have written very little about themselves, and what there is they have written for each other, not for you and me. The same is true of undertakers, hangmen and whippet-fanciers.

You can, of course, go round talking to friers; and I have done. But they are busy people, inclined to be at their busiest at those very moments—that is, mealtimes—when the visitor wants to engage them in conversation. If they have got a moment to spare, they tend to become suspicious. Are you a Public Health Inspector? Or from the Immigration Office? A plain clothes detective? A pickled eggs salesman? A tax man? Or, worst of all, some smart-aleck journalist working on a snide piece about Fish & Chips? It takes patience on both sides to establish confidence, and I am grateful to those who trusted me in the end.

Writing to friers is even worse than talking to them. With two or three notable exceptions, I might as well have used my postage stamps to keep the wind out. Of the twenty short questionnaires that I sent to local association secretaries (with stamped and addressed envelopes for return), only four came back. Not that I blame the silent friers. Questionnaires can be an impertinent nuisance these days, and they were obviously no way to collect material for this book.

One of the glories of England is its technical, trade and specialist Press. One of the best collections I know used to be laid out in the waiting-room of the British Embassy in Ankara, where loitering Turks could be subtly brain-washed by such subversive periodicals as *The Ceramic Digest, Corsetry & Underwear, Freight News Weekly, The Funeral*

Service Journal and (I swear by my fez) *The Muck Shifter*. As one brought up on the Fancy Mice Column in *Fur and Feather* (together with *The Amateur Aquarist and Reptilian Gazette*), I knew that somewhere amidst all this paper was a journal which the dedicated fish frier would as soon miss as the addicted angler would go without his monthly dose of *Rod and Line*. In fact, there were two such journals. I set forth in search of them.

The city of Leeds has a fair claim to being the intellectual capital of Fish & Chips. As you approach by train, it appears dignified and rather Lowry-esque, with a mixed skyline of spires and chimney-stacks, mysterious industrial sheds, a network of railways to all parts, and transplants of modern tower-blocks. On a sunny day it's not at all bad; on a wet day, it's satanic.

Outside the station, four naked bronze ladies called 'Morn' confront four naked bronze ladies called 'Even'. A girl with tawny hair wiggles past in provocative hot-pants. A handsome negress in fishnet tights descends, *dea ex machina*, from a green Corporation bus. What are we thinking of? After ten minutes in the bus, turning through a bombed landscape attributed to slum clearance, I find myself at 289 Dewsbury Road, headquarters of the National Federation of Fish Friers, and editorial office of its journal—my *sine qua non*—*The Fish Friers Review*, 15p. Monthly.

To postpone, for a moment, the pleasure of opening those pages: if you cross the road opposite the fire station, turning left along Dewsbury Road from Federation House, you will come soon to a whiff from Mr. W. Hemingway's Crescent Fisheries. It is a block off the main road at the intersection of Woodview Road and Woodview Street round the corner from Woodview Grove. All three are terraces of dark crimson brick with cream paintwork, bearing chimney pots with teeth and toast-rack T.V. aerials. Outside the shop an oriental lady is calling to two little girls in Punjabi trousers. Inside, Mr. Hemingway and three jolly women are shovelling away in a small, bright shop with white tiles and blue decorations. It is open for dinner, tea and supper sessions; never on Sundays; two sessions out of the three on every other day except Wednesday when there's only one.

The Special haddock is (or was) 8½p., haddock 6p., chips 3½p., and there are fishcakes (a lump of fish skewered between two slices of potato) and minerals, too. My Special with chips and a warm cola costs 15p., which is exceedingly good value. In London I should have paid 25p. It is a trifle greasy, which is my fault for not letting it settle a while, but the portions are generous and the batter is not inflationary. The editor of *The Fish Friers Review* gets his lunch in character. I find him eating it over the Book of Numbers, in his office. The youthful editor, Brian Ashurst, is one of those canny journalists who, eschewing the bitter sweets of Fleet Street, has marked out for himself a more limited sphere in which his knowledge is virtually complete and his influence all-pervasive. It also gives him room to indulge his passion for restoring and operating a nearby unnationalized railway. Behind him stretch the files of the *Review*—or *The National Fish Caterers Review* as it was in Vol. 1. No. 1. on 4th April, 1925.

Thumbing through the bound volumes, I note that in 1928 you could buy a frying range for as little as £50; they are twenty times that now. And in December 1928, the editor was complaining about the Motor Car. Instead of spending their money on nourishing Fish & Chips, he complained, people were driving off in motor cars, cooking their meals under hedges and leaving a mess behind. 'This class of people' he lectured, 'used to purchase your Fish & Chips until they grew out of it and purchased a car; or perhaps they got it on the "hire system" which made it impossible for them to afford Fish & Chips . . .' Just as bad, in the Editor's view, were the new rich, brought up decently enough to eat Fish & Chips but now 'only eating them in restaurants'. The editor advised his readers to avoid dinginess. It was impossible for a frier to look too smart.

Inevitably the editor got letters—cries from the heart of his oppressed people. 'When I think,' cried one of them, 'of all the long hours of work, worrying and trying so hard to please to create a goodwill, something that can't be seen or (as I used to think) touched, it hurts a good deal to think it's now a taxable item. It appears that if you work hard and save and use your spare time, swotting in order to better yourself and perhaps use your hard-earned assets to run a small business, you are regarded as some kind of bloated baron, oozing money, who ought to be got at.'

August 1949 found the *Review* suddenly celebrating the Centenary of the Frying Trade, for no good historical reason. 'The big difficulty', said the editor, 'is that nobody is quite certain *when* the trade could really be said to begin. Diligent research has failed to unearth any earlier reference to fish-frying as a separate trade than that made by Charles Dickens in his book *Oliver Twist*. What we do know, then, is that the trade was sufficiently well established by 1850 . . .'

In fact, the editor erred on the side of caution. But nothing could restrain the flow of editorial eloquence now: 'Did they dream, as they fried their fish (the leftovers from the fishmongers!) and as the evil-smelling oil fumes belched forth unchecked (oil was not deodorized in those days!)—did they ever dream that the day would come when the hygienic standards of the trade would set an example to all other food distributors? Impossible!'

Well, hardly contestable. But it is certainly impossible to dispense with *The Fish Friers Review*. With its columns by the editor, by Commoner (whose elder son is vice-consul in Addis Ababa) and by the archly-named Molly Codling; with its political analysis ('E.E.C. Fish Agreement Best Obtainable'—'Government Backs Friers over Icelandic Limits'); with its sensational news breaks ('Haggis penetrates South to Cornwall'—'Wiggly Chips War Flares at Basildon'—'Merchants Madden Medway Members') and with its literally seductive advertisements for batter and frying fats (my own favourite, though, is for the 'Crypto-Peerless Steam Heat Rotapan—for mouthwatering curries, chicken, puds, saveloys and peas . . .')—ah, how can one compress the riches of the *Review* into a single paragraph?

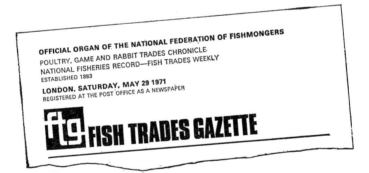

OFFICIAL ORGAN OF THE NATIONAL FEDERATION OF FISHMONGERS
POULTRY, GAME AND RABBIT TRADES CHRONICLE
NATIONAL FISHERIES RECORD—FISH TRADES WEEKLY
ESTABLISHED 1883
LONDON, SATURDAY, MAY 29 1971
REGISTERED AT THE POST OFFICE AS A NEWSPAPER

FISH TRADES GAZETTE

But for all its merits and its domination of the frying readership of today, the *Review* is not, in fact, the senior journal in the field. That distinction belongs to the ninety-year-old *Fish Trades Gazette*, which is weekly, similar in appearance, though smaller in page size and page numbers. After a dispute with the friers in 1940, the *Gazette* came down on the fish*mongers*' side of the fence, where it had originally started, and it is now the official organ of their Federation. But it would have been foolish for it to neglect the friers, since their numbers are steady while those of the 'mongers fall; and so the *Gazette* still offers regular titbits to entice the frier. There are extensive small ads., articles by officials of the Friers' Federation, and news stories like 'Keen Fish and Chips mayor finds plenty of interest in Medway frying exhibition'.

The *Gazette* is essentially a Southern institution, an offshoot of Billingsgate. It is part of the Industrial Newspapers group, and issues from a building in John Adam Street which runs parallel with the Strand between Charing Cross and the Embankment Gardens. Its editor, Graham Large, is much of an age, and one might say much of a kind, with his competitor Brian Ashurst; though Large is an ounce or two less grave, and less inclined to eat Fish & Chips at his desk as a matter of duty.

Across the road from his office—precisely where, I do not propose to reveal, for reasons of security—is a basement annexe which houses, besides a charming gentleman who devotes his life to the journalism of crockery, the back files of the *Gazette* and sundry other technical contemporaries. The discoverers of the tomb of Tutankhamun can have experienced no greater thrill than the researcher who first dips into those dusty pages. The difficulty is to keep anywhere near the straight and narrow path of Fish & Chips; for glaring up from the very first issue, on 26th May 1883, is:

THE TRUTH ABOUT MONTE CARLO!
The gambling at Monte Carlo, long a disgrace to the Principality, is now admittedly a gross scandal to the civilized world, and the movement for its suppression increases in strength and influence every year . . . The average Englishman who takes his family thither does not know the class of people by whom his olive branches arc surrounded; he cannot be expected to detect the *cocottes* and *decaves* in the fashionably dressed women and the sleek well-groomed men who cluster round the tables, and who form a large proportion of the *habitues* and patrons of this real 'hell upon earth' . . .

Olive branches? And whatever can be a *decave*? But *revenons à nos poissons*. The small advertisements on the front pages of these early *Gazettes* are bursting with information. These, from the issue of 29th September 1883, for example:

FISH (Fried, Wet and Dried) and Potatoes; thickly populated neighbourhood; no opposition; smoke-hole and every convenience; price low. 12 Moody St., Bancroft Rd., E.

FISH (Fried) Business; crowded neighbourhood; rare opportunity;

price for everything £25. Apply Mr. Daltrey, 14 Monier Rd., Old Ford.

FISH Supper Bar, Alamode Potatoes and Stewed Eel Business; thickly populated neighbourhood; proprietor having met with a serious accident, cause of leaving. 10 Bedford Street, Commercial Rd.

FISH (Dried, Fried) and Potatoes. East End Shop doing £26 weekly which could easily be doubled by an energetic man. Lease 20 years, Rent £40. Thomas Mogg, Shoreditch.

There are a number of shops to rent for ten shillings a week, and several which claim to have been in the same hands for up to twenty-five years, which would take us back to 1858. But the advertising of Fried Fish shops is soon discontinued, and there is virtually no mention of the Trade in the *Gazette* for almost twenty years. One senses that the subject had been ruled *infra dig.* and unrewarding for a journal which was concentrating on the more genteel readership of Billingsgate and the High Street fishmongers.

Not that the *Gazette* pulled its editorial punches: 'Why', it demands in October 1884, 'in these days of refrigerators and cheap ice should 86 tons of fish at Billingsgate be allowed to become unfit for human food, in one month?' The *Gazette* wages an unrelenting war against the railways, blaming them for carrying fish 'only as a sort of obligatory abomination. They have treated the traders with the most meagre amount of respect it is possible for one class of human beings to show to another—being, in fact, little short of the savagery of a negro-driver to his slaves.' All one can add is (sic).

The early *Gazette* has a roving eye for fishy sensation. There are headlines crying 'Audacious Fish Fraud' and 'Great Kipper Scandal'. Besides a constant concern for the Native Oyster and Shrimp ('We cry aloud for justice for the British Shrimp, or rather—whether Midlothian likes it or not—for justice to the *English* Shrimp!'), the magazine treats the American and Canadian fisheries as if they were virtual provinces of the North Sea. In July 1886 it reports 'Terrible Mortality and Cannibalism' in Labrador. 'The Indians in that locality are eating their dead companions. Those who died among the white settlers are buried secretly to keep the Esquimaux from getting their bodies. The graves are all disguised.' A year or two later the *Gazette* announces succinctly and without further explanation: 'A shower of fish fell in Indiana.'

On 15th June 1895, the *Gazette* was airing another of its pet prejudices: 'A man has died at Skipton, Bradford, from eating tinned salmon', it announced. Not so long ago there had been a glut of salmon on the market. Changing the subject: 'Do Fishes Sleep? I think there can be no doubt that fishes sleep, says Mr. Mattias Dunn . . .'

My own favourite item from the *Gazette* appeared in 1909, under the headline 'Alleged Cruelty to Eels'. It was a case, brought by the Royal Society for the Prevention of Cruelty to Animals, vividly calling to mind the episode in the autumn of 1971, when the electrocution of thirty-five catfish at the Hayward Gallery in London (it was said to be part of an Ecological Art Event) had to be called off following denunciations by the R.S.P.C.A. and the breaking of glass by Mr. Spike Milligan. The earlier case actually came to trial. A Lavender Hill fishmonger was charged with 'causing unnecessary suffering to certain wild animals in captivity, to wit: seven eels.' There was much debate about whether eels *were* animals, whether they really suffered at all after their heads were cut off, and whether similar charges might not be brought against the oyster-openers at the Savoy. The case was dismissed after the magistrate had told a long and revolting story about human heads biting each other in the basket beneath the Guillotine. Thirty years later, my wife was still taking her little brother and sister for an afternoon's Grand Guignol, watching the headless eels writhe on a stall in Brixton.

It was in 1904 that *The Fish Trades Gazette* decided to readmit the friers to polite society—an indication of how the Trade was progressing. An advertisement appeared for 'a capable man' to do a weekly column of use and interest to friers; and within a month the series began with an article on the legal aspects of running a fried fish shop. They were signed 'A London Frier', and in September 1904 the *Gazette* announced that arrangements would be made to publish the series in the form of a book, to be entitled *How to Create a Successful Fried Fish Business*. This would have been, in effect, the Old Testament of the Trade; but I can find no evidence that it actually appeared.

The series, however, stands in bound volumes of the *Gazette*, and it is full of sage advice to friers, like not making a display of fish in the window. This may, says A London Frier, put people off, especially if you are frying 'imitation fish—I include under this nickname Catfish, Dogfish, Tusks, Weavers, Gurnets, Monks, Saithe and other fish of the kind sold to

Titbit from 1905 Fish Trades Gazette

Frog-Caviar.—According to a German journal a new industry appears to be springing up in Russia, owing to the high price of the proper caviar, which as everyone knows is prepared from the eggs of the sturgeon. The spawn of frogs is now being collected by a French factory and made into caviar.

the public as anything from Whiting to Sturgeon. You would not be able to display any of these kinds of ugly fish to any advantage, and that is why I recommend painted windows with standing advertisements. It is also well to have in your shop Music Hall or Theatre bills, for your customers' perusal while waiting for fish . . .' Catfish, dogfish, monkfish and saithe are still in use today, pieces of monkfish sometimes masquerading tastily as scampi; but it is odd to find weaverfish on the menu. It has poisonous spines.

A London Frier shares the *Gazette*'s low opinion of fish by rail: 'How many cases are there,' he demands, 'of vanloads of unsold fish being sent back to the different stations, only to be taken to market again next morning? I have known them to be taken backwards and forwards for three days before being cleared . . .'

Some years later, on 7th August 1909, occurred one of the key moments of the saga of our subject: the first appearance of the first article in a series entitled 'The Fish Frier and His Trade (How to Establish and Carry on an Up-to-Date Business)'. The author was a Sheffield-born frier called William Loftas, writing under the pseudonym of Chatchip.

From the start, fish journalism had had a peculiar addiction to *noms de plume*. The earliest *Gazette* had a columnist called Anchovy Sauce, though he was soon replaced by Dorsal Fin (occasionally Caudal Fin) and Observant. Through later pages of both the *Gazette* and the *Review* swim the disguised figures of Macte-Animo and Frier Tuck (ho-ho-ho!), of Reformer and Commoner, Molly Codling and Crispo, Chipbasket and The Hermit of Guernsey, Lobster Pott and Two Penn'orth. But none, I think, will ever match in longevity, experience and single-minded dedication to his craft the sweep of Chatchip. He was still writing in 1949, but his masterwork, the refined and collected articles, appeared in 1924 as *The Fish Frier and His Trade—A complete Compendium to the Arts and Appliances of the Fried Fish Trade, together with much other useful information relating thereto—Published by E. Hyde & Sons (The Fish Trades Gazette)—Illustrated*. Chatchip (or Loftas, if you will) drew upon this work in a series he wrote for the *Review*'s pseudo-centenary issue of 1949. But the *fons et origo* remains the *Gazette* series of 1909, with its opening words: 'Probably in the whole history of trades there is none which had so humble and unpleasant a beginning as the fried fish trade . . .', a promise to which Chatchip fully lives up, or rather, down.

Chatchip has very little competition. In 1933 there appeared in two volumes *The Modern Fish Frier* by H. T. Reeves (author of *Potato Crisps, Modern Frying Methods, The Modern Fish Restaurant*, etc.), published by Harrap. But Reeves, for all his practical advice about coal sizes and his up-to-dateness ('nothing is more objectionable than paraffin in close contact with food'), is lacking in historical perspective, proletarian solidarity and soul; he is a handbook, but not a Bible.

After that, just a stepping-stone here and there. Charles L. Cutting, B.Sc., Ph.D., F.R.I.C., is to be commended for a chapter in his *Fish Saving* (Leonard Hill, 1955), outlining some of the early history of Fish & Chip shops, even though it does perpetuate an error about the publication of *Oliver Twist*. Cutting emphasizes Fish & Chips' role as a method of *preserving* fish which was convenient for the middle Industrial Revolution.

Greville Havenhand (whom God preserve) nibbles at the Trade for one chapter of his 1970 *A Nation of Shopkeepers*, fitting it into the pattern of 'the Retail Revolution'. But his chip shop is really the odd man out, crying for a study of its own. And it shall have one.

5. Fish meets Chips

The scene is set, a marriage has been arranged. But when? And where? It is one thing to trace the development of Fried Fish, another to uncover the descent of Fried Potatoes, a third to bring them together and a fourth to determine whether they are legitimately united as the Fish & Chips we recognize today.

In the second paragraph of Chapter 26 in *Oliver Twist*, Charles Dickens writes: 'Near to the spot on which Snow Hill and Holborn Hill meet, there opens, upon the right hand as you come out of the City, a narrow and dismal alley leading to Saffron Hill . . .' This was the thieves' market frequented by Fagin, and Dickens continues: 'Confined as the limits of Field Lane are, it has its barber, its coffee-shop, its beer-shop, and its fried-fish warehouse . . .'

This is the classic first mention of fried fish as a prepared Convenience Food. For some reason, it has been accepted and perpetuated in the newspaper cuttings files as dating from 1851 (the year of the Great Exhibition); but the fact is, *Oliver Twist* was published in instalments between 1837 and 1839; so that it would not be unreasonable to date the London fried fish business from, at the latest, the mid-1830s—twenty years or so earlier than usually assumed. The alley, Field Lane, is marked clearly on Rocque's Atlas of 1746, and in 1840 an engraving was made of it, with signs hanging over the street reading 'Scrooge's' and 'Fagan's' (sic), probably artist's licence. But by 1880, Field Lane was recorded as 'lately improved out of existence', and today, if there is any trace of it left at all it must be at the bottom end of Saffron Hill. It certainly is a 'narrow and dismal alley', still partly cobbled; but it is inhabited not by shoe vampers and petty thieves, but by respectable lithographers, a company of window-cleaners, 'Champion Catering Machines'—and a *cheese* warehouse. Of fish there is not a whiff.

Between 1799 and 1823, the supply of North Sea fish reaching Billingsgate Market had risen from 2,500 tons a year to 12,000 tons (not to mention 500 million oysters). The fleets of Grimsby, Brixham, Ramsgate and Barking were active, and plaice had become so common they had ceased to be a delicacy and were sometimes tossed back into the sea, along with the unwanted haddock and whiting. Ice, although available, did not filter down to places like Field Lane, however, and the object of frying was not so much to provide the working classes with a ready-to-eat hot meal, but to kill the smell of stale and inferior fish and preserve it for a day or two longer while it was disposed of cheap and cold.

Modern contrast: 1971 prices

FRYING TIMES

TUES TO SAT

11 A.M. TO 1.30 P.M.

7.30 P.M. TO 11 P.M.

COD	FROM	6½P
HADDOCK		9
PLAICE		9
SKATE		11
COD ROE		5
BEEFBURGER		6
CORNISH PASTIE		5½
CHIPS		4
PEA FRITTER		2
FISHCAKE		2½
SAUSAGE		2½
CHICKEN		15
COTTAGE PIE		14

Sir Shirley Murphy, who was in 1906 the London County Council's Medical Officer of Health, records that there were 'a few fried fish shops' in the year of the Great Exhibition. At that time, he says, the fish was commonly sold in conjunction with *baked* potatoes, or with bread, adding: 'The trade is said to have been well-nigh revolutionized about thirty-five years ago [*i.e. c.*1870], when the practice of combining the sale of fried fish with that of *à la mode* or chipped potatoes was introduced from France.'

But chronologically, our next major source of information is Henry Mayhew's *London Labour and the London Poor* of 1861. Mayhew estimates there were some three hundred friers in the city at that time and talks to one who has been in the trade since about 1843—which, incidentally, Mayhew also takes as about the earliest date for the birth of the baked potato trade. The potatoes, it appears, were taken to a bread-baker's one-quarter boiled, to be finished off in the oven at 9d. a hundredweight. They were then taken away wrapped in green baize and installed in a four-legged potato-heater containing a charcoal firepot. There was one formidable machine in Shoreditch which had cost ten guineas 'and is of brass mounted with German silver. There are three lamps attached to it, with coloured glass and of a style to accord with that of the machine.' Butter and salt were available for the customers, and I, for one, greatly lament the passing of this warming and nutritious commodity. It is hard to counterfeit the honest baked potato, but who knows what goes into the dubious British Hot Dog?

Mayhew's frier sold bread or nothing with his fish, which were 'dabs' — small plaice or sole, the 'overplus of the fishmonger's stores—of what he has not sold overnight and does not care to offer for sale the following morning.' The fish was washed, gutted and trimmed (but not filleted), then dipped in flour and water (indicating that batter was already in use to bind and disguise the fish), and fried in oil 'in ordinary frying pans'. Thus it was not yet being deep-fried. Mayhew's frier had started by taking seven to ten shillings a night gross and making a profit of thirty shillings a week, 'a good mechanic's earning'. Later his wife opened a stall and they doubled their earnings. Publicans allowed him to hawk fish round their taverns, crying 'Fish and Bread, a penny!', and people would stand *rounds* of fish to their friends; but lately, said the frier, 'The insults and difficulties I've had in the public houses trade is dreadful'.

All that was really needed for the itinerant trade was a neatly painted wooden tray slung from the neck by a leather strap, a pile of clean newspaper spread with from twenty to sixty lumps of fish, a garnish of parsley and a salt-box. One could set up in business for ten shillings, or for as little as one shilling with second-hand gear.

Mayhew reported: 'The fried fish sellers live in some out-of-the-way alley, and not infrequently in garrets, for even among the poorest class there are great objections to their being fellow-lodgers on account of the odour of the frying.' There were hotbeds of friers around Gray's Inn Lane and Leather Lane, between Fetter Lane and Chancery Lane; also around Smithfield and Clerkenwell, Bishopsgate Street and Kingsland Road, and 'in the half-ruinous buildings near the Southwark and Borough Roads'. One man told Mayhew, in a phrase that has haunted and taunted the Trade ever since: 'A gin-drinking neighbourhood suits best, for people haven't their smell so correct there.'

So there we are, as far as London is concerned, in the year 1861, with Fish and no Chips. In 1883 (inspired by the Great London Fisheries Exhibition of that year) Edward Forester Hyde launches the *Gazette*; and there on the front page are 'For Sale' advertisements for Fried Fish and Potato Shops, or in some cases Fried Fish and *Alamode* businesses. Some of them claim to go as far back as the fifties, but it does not follow that they had always sold both fish *and* chips, or that their fried potatoes were chips. Some old London friers have told me that, as late as the early 1900s, there were shops in the East End selling small potatoes fried whole (like the delicious *Pommes Frites* one used to get in the Haute Savoie), or else chunks and slices, and that in most cases the peeling was rudimentary. There is also much evidence that shops commonly began by selling wet fish, greengroceries or tripe. It is significant that the helpful Chatchip expresses the view that Fish & Chips cannot really be combined with anything else *but* Tripe. He gives two reasons: because Tripe makes 'a very decent window display', and because in a good-class neighbourhood, people who would rather die than admit to patronizing a Fish & Chip shop have no hesitation in telling the neighbours they are 'off to the tripe merchant's'.

We are left with this gap between the years 1860 and 1880; but to fill it, we must take a leap forward in time. In 1965 *The Fish Friers Review* launched yet another attempt to celebrate the centenary of the Trade. But it took three years for the Friers' Federation to agree on symbolic evidence—the identity of the Oldest Fish & Chip Shop in the World, preferably one at least a hundred years old.

After much inquiry and not a little lobbying, the lot fell upon Malin's of 560 Old Ford Road, now the possessors of a plaque which reads:

The World's Oldest
Fish and Chip Business
MALIN'S
Presented 1968 by the
National Federation of Fish Friers
to mark
100 Years of Fish and Chips.

Top   London's oldest chip-shop: in the middle, Malin's
Bottom   The Malins: Father, Grandfather, Son. A century of frying

John Rouse's 'Dandy': first on the road in 1880

Top Early 'Acme' coal-cum-gas range. Note optional aspidistras
Bottom Nuttall's float in 1920s Rochdale carnival. Note optional
potted palms

H. P. Crump's *circa* 1914. Fish fried to order *and all potatoes peeled*

Malin's present establishment, under hourly threat of demolition by slum clearance contractors, has an undistinguished frontage between a café and a betting shop. Council housing, some of it fifteen stories high and more, looms all around, interspersed with timber-yards, canals, the approaches to the Blackwall Tunnel and the undervalued greenery of Victoria Park. The Malin family are Cornish in origin. Albert Malin, who was seventy-eight when I met him, and still frying one day a week to keep his hand in, *thought* the business was founded in 1860 (or was it 1865?) by his Great Grandfather or his Great Uncle Joe (though it is possible we may have a 'Great' too many in here). Anyway, Albert Malin was born over a fish shop at 103, Old Bethnal Green Road, soon moved to the family's original establishment in 'Cleveland Street' (which must surely be Cleveland *Way*), and then to another at Goldsmith's Row—all in the Stepney-Bethnal Green neighbourhood. Finally he settled at the Old Ford site, which had joined the Malin network in 1884.

By a miracle, one of this shop's original customers, ninety-eight-year-old George Mayston was still alive, and collecting his daily order, when I visited Old Ford. Mr. Mayston recalled that when his family moved from Islington 'we didn't know what Fish and Chips was . . .'; but from the age of ten 'I used to get a ha'penny piece of fish and a ha'porth of chips for myself, the same for my sister, and three-ha'penny pieces with a ha'porth of chips each for my mother and father. I think myself the chips in those days used to be more on the crispy side . . . We had the skin left on the chips . . . There used to be fish shops coming up like mushrooms in those days.'

So there we have proof of Fish and unpeeled Chips in 1884, and unshakeable faith in the business stretching back into the sixties. With

Victorian scoops: durable designs

CHIP LIFTER.

Wire gauze sieve is of similar construction, but of an exceedingly fine mesh.

CHIP SERVING SCOOP.

FISH SLICER OR LIFTER.

Albert Malin's son Denis, and *his* son Graham, still in the Trade at the Old Ford address, the evidence for Malin's being the oldest continuous business of its kind is impressive but not entirely bullet-proof. The same, however, is true of most of its rivals. When the plaque was handed over to Denis Malin at a ceremony patronized by the Friers Federation, the W.F.A., the Potato Board and the Minister of Agriculture and Fisheries in person, there was some indignant sniping from the North. What, demanded the, rebels, about Lees' up at Mossley, in Lancashire?

To get to Mossley (which is pronounced 'Mozzley') you go to Manchester and ride out along Ashton Old Road, which looks as if it had recently been gutted by a race riot. More slum clearance. Mossley itself is a grey hillside town bathed in a smoky, opalescent light, with black and white cows on the surrounding heights. It used to be a weaving and spinning town, but today one of the mills is a broiler-chicken factory, another makes handbag frames and a third, candlewick bedspreads. The terraced cottages still groan under the weight of their flagstone roofs, but some of the old folk are grousing about the council's insistence on improving them by installing central heating. Twelve weeks it takes. It is the invasion of their privacy by strangers that they really resent.

It is many years since Lees' was in fact run by a member of the Lees family, so the blood link has gone anyway. But eighty-year old Joe Lees, who quit in 1943, is the grandson of the founder, John Lees, and remembers him well. Here again, the evidence is mostly oral tradition, and it goes like this:

In 1863, John Lees (then about twenty-eight) set up a little wooden hut on the market ground opposite the Stamford Arms public house. From this hut, he and his wife competed with the next-door tripe-seller (a Mr. Beswick) by selling pea-soup with pigs trotters. One day, John Lees visited Oldham, where he found a man selling 'chipped potatoes in the French style'. All else we know of this man is that he later ran a pub called The White Bear—'but it's been demolished years ago'. Lees returned to Mossley impressed, and added the delicacy to his menu. Over the little wooden hut it now said 'Chipped Potatoes in the French and American Style'. Where the American Style came in, Joe Lees has no idea; 'It were a gimmick', he supposes. But there really *is* no American style, unless it be what Americans call 'French fries', which brings us back full circle.

The important thing about this tale so far is that *there was no mention of fish*. Nor was there any when the wooden huts were torn down in 1897 (Joe remembers carrying off the wreckage for firewood), and the Lees moved immediately across the road into a former sweet shop. A photograph taken at the time of the Coronation in 1902 shows it already displaying its boast as 'The Oldest Chip Potato Establishment in the

World'. It is worth noting that, as a rule, Yorkshire and the rest of Britain talk of 'fish shops', while Lancashire and to some extent Cheshire have always put the potatoes first and spoken of 'Chippers' or 'Chippies'.

The shop in Mossley, now opposite a bus stop and car park, has hardly changed at all externally in the past seventy years. The local branch of the British Legion, as a consolation for being passed over in the centenary competition, has awarded it a special plaque of its own.

What intrigues me most about this evidence is the reference to the man in Oldham. For Nuttalls, the Rochdale range-making firm, claimed in a *Review* article dated March 1969 that 'Fish and Chips were united in the 1860s by an Oldham tripe-dresser named Dyson', who commissioned iron-founder Harry Nuttall to make him a range. Nuttalls went on to claim they had manufactured ranges since 1866, which is remarkably early, pre-dating that of a Londoner named Teuten who started making castings for fish friers in 1869.

Nuttalls are also earlier than two other great names in the business, Rouse and Faulkner. Faulkners supplied 'quite a fair number of ranges' in the 1870s, for the frying of chips only, the company believes; while John Rouse literally got his show on the road in 1880, with the first mobile chip-range. What I take to be highly significant is that both companies were, as they still are, established in Oldham. I have little doubt that it was the two-county area between Oldham and Bradford which gave rise to the Fish & Chips industry as we now know it.

For a start, the conditions were right: the tradition of potato-eating and potato-growing reinforced by the Irish proximity; increasing supplies of fish, both from the Irish and the North Sea, brought rapidly to hand by rail; a mass market of industrial shift-workers who not only 'sent out a lad for some lunch', but among whom there were many housewives with little time to prepare a hot meal for their family at home. And there was money; not a lot, but enough to buy a meal out, or indulge the craving for an extra snack. Here in the small, closely knit mill towns, with the warmth of their street cultures, their working-class solidarity, strong community spirit and insistence on knowing and being known, here rather than in shifting London were the conditions for the true family Fish & Chip business to develop.

A key figure in this hypothesis, the Betsy Ross of Fish & Chips, and a link between North and South, is that of 'Granny' Duce. 'Granny' came from Bradford, where prior to 1880 she had two or three combined greengrocery-plus-Fish-&-Chips shops. Both the elders among her descendants, and Messrs. Faulkners who supplied her with ranges, are emphatic that Fish *and* Chips issued from those establishments before she came South; although, seeing that she was born in 1847, the legend of her having put the combination together in 1864, when she would only have been seventeen, is open to doubt. One can no more *prove* that

'Granny' invented Fish & Chips than that Dyson the tripe-dresser did. We know that chips were often sold by tripe-dressers, and that people sometimes brought cold pieces of fried fish to the chip shops to be warmed up by a quick plunge in the boiling fat. The combination must have occurred on and off to quite a number of people.

Some time in the 1880s, 'Granny' Duce's husband—a railwayman and not a frier—was transferred to duty at Watford. 'Granny' sold up in Bradford, came South with him and repeated her Fish & Chip operation there. In addition to the main shop in Watford High Street (the premises have now changed use), there developed a chain of Duce's Fish Cafés all the way from Aylesbury to Hazlemere. 'Granny's' economical management left enough money, upon her death in 1933, to set up a whole flock of children and grandchildren in business. The leadership of the clan has now passed to Mr. B. H. Baldwin, a relative by marriage, and its headquarters is in High Wycombe.

There is no doubt in my mind that Mrs. Duce was selling Fish *and* Chips in Bradford long before John Lees was selling them in Mossley. But can we be sure that she anticipated Joseph Malin in London? If Malin really was frying in both kinds by 1865, then Mrs. Duce's claim looks pale. But *was* he? The evidence is unclear upon two points: first, was Malin frying potatoes at all that early? Second, if he was, was he really frying chips? Sir Shirley Murphy says that chipped 'alamode' potatoes joined the fried fish in London about 1870, but we have also seen reports that they were being sold in the North some ten years earlier. A few years ago, in a letter to *The Sunday Times*, a Liverpool reader, whom I have been unable to track down, claimed without further evidence that the trade dated back to 1781 in Lancashire. The very word 'chips' is of Northern origin so far as the frying dictionary is concerned.

Anyone who has visited a northern French seaside resort—Cherbourg comes to mind—will know that *pommes frites*, served by themselves off a barrow, are a thoroughly French outdoor snack. How far back they go I have been unable to discover, but I do not think John Lees would have boasted of his 'French style' potatoes if they did not go back earlier than 1860. London at that time was eating its potatoes baked; indeed baked potatoes continued to sell in the London streets as late as 1893; and so, it would appear, fried potatoes 'in the French style' caught on in the North somewhat earlier than they did in the South, perhaps because the North was better equipped with workshops to make the ranges.

In any event it appears that the potato 'alamode' was only a refinement of the brutally fried chunks already eaten in the North. Whether some individual French cook was responsible for bringing the good chips from Ghent to Oldham, I cannot say; it is possible; but I must reject as far too late the Scottish claim that it was really a Belgian immigrant named Eduard de Gernier, who set up his stall in Dundee in 1874. It would be delightful to be able to reproduce, out of the files of some 1815 Liverpool broadsheet, an account of how a Napoleonic prisoner of war, newly released, had been hanged for selling fried cod and fingers of Irish potato from a barrow on a Sunday. But it is the merest fantasy. No such pinpointing will ever be achieved.

For, however important a role 'Granny' Duce or Joseph Malin may have played in their development, Fish & Chips are a product, an expression of the British (and I believe *North* British) collective folk genius. If a memorial has to be erected somewhere, it might as well be on Ilkley Moor, within easy reach of Harry Ramsden's Chip 'oile.

6. An Offensive Trade

(Author's note: certain descriptions quoted in this chapter employ a frankness of language which some readers may wish to be spared.)

he glory of frying is that of all modes of cookery it enlists or evokes the maximum number of senses at once. All but the deaf must enjoy the hissing and crackling; all but the blind, the progressive browning; all but those without noses, the promise of the aroma; and all but the unweaned, the intimations of hot-toothed crispness. The trouble is, as anyone knows who has ever fried fish at home, frying requires a nice judgment of temperature if the food is to be properly cooked without making the house smell like one of Mayhew's back alleys. There are few homes in Britain today where the spirit of the Fried Fish does not linger for a good hour or more after the last bones have been scraped from the plate. So it is no small tribute to the modern frier that he can serve scores of customers every day (except Sunday), without being suppressed as a public nuisance. Some, in fact, *are* suppressed—though the latest I know about was an American Fried Chicken Parlor in Belsize Park. Complaints are usually rare these days.

It was not always so. For one thing, the public demand to have its fish served fried was not to be diverted. In a footnote to one of the handbooks to the Great London Fisheries Exhibition of 1883, we find a writer complaining that 'notwithstanding the efforts of the accomplished lady superintendent to introduce to the public new modes of cooking fish, curries, stews, etc., she informs me that these have been entirely neglected, and among the thousands or more daily visitors to the fish restaurant, three-fourths demand *fried* fish and the other fourth take it steamed.'

The Exhibition's catalogues are entirely lacking in any mention of deep-frying or chip-making apparatus. But it is quite clear that London's poor, though reluctant to accept fish in the workhouse, were already tucking into Fish & Chips in the street, even if it had to be supplied in the main from adapted clothes coppers and soap boilers.

The goods may have been popular, but the friers were not. Mayhew, back in 1861, had remarked that the friers were not popular as lodgers, because of their smell; and in 1876 a pioneering report by a public health inspector named Dr. Ballard summed up the Trade as follows:

Salford, circa *1870. Stench radius:* ¼ *mile*

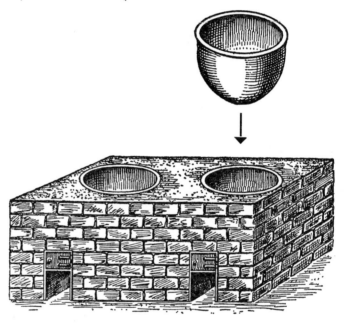

'It is a petty trade, but, nevertheless, it is a source of considerable nuisance in some neighbourhoods, the offensive smell of the oil boiling and the fish frying spreading often through the whole length of the street where the shop is situated, and sometimes into the adjoining streets also. When a shop is situated in a street occupied by poor persons of the class who purchase such food, complaints of the smell are rarely, if ever, made; but pedestrians are annoyed by it, and so also are the tenants of houses of the better class who chance to reside in the neighbourhood. For it is not only in poor streets that such shops are to be found. There is, I believe, scarcely a health officer in London who has not at some time been called upon by the authority under which he acts to advise as to an appropriate remedy for this nuisance.'

The oil, which seems to have been the main offender, was mostly cottonseed oil (except where mutton fat or beef dripping was used).

Oil was a by-product of textile cotton, but it was not until the early 1900s that a way was found to deodorize it by treating it with caustic potash and superheated steam. The finest Egyptian cottonseed oil was rather better than the usual American variety, but as a whole it was a vile medium before deodorization.

Thirty years after Ballard's report, things had somewhat improved because, although the number of friers had increased greatly, so had the force of inspectors. In 1906, Sir Shirley Murphy of the London County Council reported that his men had, during the previous year, visited 1,053 premises, more than two-thirds of the estimated total in London. It might have been expected, said Sir Shirley, that as the Trade gradually emerged from the obscure back alleys of which Mayhew had spoken, more and more objections might have been raised on the score of nuisance. But 'concurrently with the extension of its appeal to class after class, rising in the social scale, improvements have gradually been introduced, and in many respects the trade has been transformed from what it was in those early days . . .'

However, it was not the 'offensive vapours' noted by Sir Shirley that mattered so much as 'the risk of contamination of the fish itself', and what the public eye did not see, the L.C.C.'s heart grieved over very deeply. Sir Shirley went on: 'The conditions under which fish is cleansed and stored are, as a rule, most unsatisfactory . . . Numerous instances were found in which floors and walls were fouled with decomposing fish slime and excremental matter, and the portion of the wall adjoining the bench on which cleansing and gutting of the fish was effected was that commonly found to be at fault. Frying and cleansing were carried on in basements, badly lighted, ill-ventilated and in a filthy condition . . . putrid and offensive . . . stagnant and odorous pools of water were observed . . .'

Sir Shirley Murphy recommended the use of large metal hoods over the frying ranges, to draw the steam and the vapours away up the flue. Many installed them. But Chatchip, the immortal, who was just starting his column in the *Gazette* denounced them as 'hiding places for matter of a revolting character which is slowly but steadily becoming putrid. Most London friers still love their hoods,' he added, with a hygienic Northern shudder, 'but notwithstanding their costliness and the efforts made to make them look pretty, they are neither useful nor ornamental, and underneath many of them there are enough poisonous substances to kill the whole population within the Metropolitan Police Area.'

The Public Health Act of 1875—amended in 1891, 1896 and 1907—laid down a fine of £50, plus a further £2 a day for continued transgression, for conducting the 'Offensive Trades' of blood-boiler, bone-boiler, fell-monger (i.e. dealer in slaughtered hides), soap-boiler, tallow-melter or tripe-boiler, without official authorization. None of the Acts specified fish-frying as such; but one of them did mention 'any other noxious or offensive trade which the Local Authority may declare by order (confirmed by the Local Government Board) to be an Offensive Trade.' A number of well-bred authorities pricked up their nostrils. But should fish-frying come permanently within such a category, just because it could *sometimes* be offensive, when badly conducted?

The Fish Trades Gazette, always inclined towards gentility, rather let the side down, its new columnist writing: 'I am sorry to say that some shops smell so bad that people class them all alike. I have often seen people turn up their noses and cross over to the other side of the street. This is simply caused by common oil or fat.' And the writer went on to deliver a stern warning against the economy of buying second-hand dripping from boarding houses, which had already used it two or three times.

1880–1920. Note iron hood and fish-holder

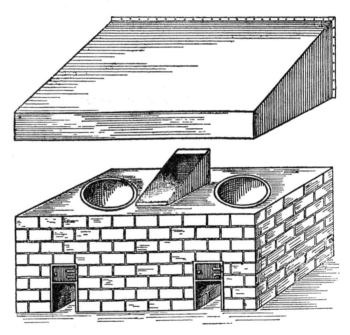

Evidently the *Gazette* thought the most effective form of defence should begin by conceding the attack. Apologetically it argued: 'Although the majority of fried fish shops are now defective in construction and not as clean as they should be . . . many improvements have been made recently, particularly during the last four years. The shops are, on this account, further appreciated by the public and used by a better class to a great extent.' The attentive Chatchip joined in, deploring the custom of attributing the taste for Fish & Chips solely to the poor. Many fried fish shops, he claimed, could boast among their regular patrons city councillors, magistrates, clergymen, ministers, business proprietors and managers, 'as well as hosts of respectable and intelligent working people'. And he hinted menacingly at rumours that, across the Channel, the Government of France was making strenuous efforts to reproduce the British Fish & Chips Industry.

But the blood of the bourgeoisie was up and the papers began to fill with reports of babies poisoned by eating chips, mothers snatched from their families by a mouthful of putrid hake, breadwinners crippled for life (in Walsall) by fish dinners from unwholesome shops.

Week by week, Chatchip fought valiantly back. *The Pall Mall Gazette* ('not a poor man's paper') had been reviving the antagonism towards the friers by complaining of widespread and ill-defined smells. But, retorted the ecologically advanced Chatchip, 'It is not only the fish smells nuisance that ought to be stopped. The abominable stink created by many readers of *The Pall Mall Gazette* as they rush through the streets of our cities and our country lanes in their motor cars, and the abominable clouds of dust and dirt they stir up and scatter about ought to be stopped, too!' Chatchip thought it an injustice and an insult to every frier in the country, to be hounded and branded as they were.

But the campaign went on. Barking, Dudley, High Wycombe, St. Albans, even Blackpool tried and too often succeeded in having Fish & Chips scheduled an Offensive Trade. Even Chatchip had some of the wind taken out of his sails when the President of the Local Government Board, John Burns, took him on a tour of London fish frying shops, pointing out to him the congealed batter on the windows and the walls. Chatchip insisted that no Northern frier would have kept a pig in such a stye as some London friers worked in.

The Minister, egged on by Sir Shirley Murphy, wanted to put the friers behind glass screens, where they could keep their batter to themselves. Some of them, he said, 'tossed it about like a gardener watering a garden'. Chatchip retorted that with his hoods and glass screens, Sir Shirley was determined to save the public even if he killed off the friers. The outcome was a great confrontation, in person, between the Minister and a deputation of six friers. It took place on Monday, 13th February 1911—a date etched for ever among the golden-brown memories of the Trade. For although the immediate result was that fish-frying *did* take its place on the list of scheduled Offensive Trades, the effect upon Chatchip and his colleagues of actually being received in Whitehall quite anæsthetized the pain. By 1912, Chatchip is congratulating the Trade in general and himself in particular for their steady rise in social standing. 'It is true to say,' he pontificates, adding a further thought, 'that the fried fish trade has done more in the cause of sobriety among our working people than all the temperance agencies combined.'

By 1914, the total of Fish & Chip shops throughout the kingdom had reached about 25,000, a number that was cut back by the War and its accompanying shortages, only to rise again shortly after the end of hostilities. During the inter-war years, however, the organized Trade felt itself at first too weak to do much about the injustice of being classed 'offensive', and then, secretly, unsure whether declassification would be such an advantage after all. For if special permission were needed no longer, then *anyone* might open a Fish & Chips shop *anywhere*; and the Trade, while theoretically founded upon free and unfettered competition, was in practice about as much in favour of it as a mediæval guild (which, at times, the National Federation has much resembled).

However, freedom struck (or appeared to strike) in the dark days of 1940, when at last *The Fish Friers Review* was able to announce:

FROM TUESDAY NEXT FISH FRYING CEASES TO BE AN OFFENSIVE TRADE
From October 1st 1940, we are no longer to be classed with bloodboilers and gut-scrapers . . .

The wartime Government, anxious to keep open as many sources as possible of off-ration food, decided that nothing should be done to hamper the friers' contribution. They were, in fact, treated better than many more genteel forms of catering, and continued to be during the early post-war years when more than a third of the 25,000 establishments were shops on wheels, serving country districts and public housing estates. The law about mobile smells was obscure.

But none of this was to last. Under the 1945 Town and Country Planning Act, Fish & Chip shops were put into a special category along with Tripe shops, Pet shops and Catsmeat butchers; and although the Trade smarted anew under this implied Untouchability, it also saw anew the advantage of not making competition too easy. As late as 1971, the National Federation was urging the planners to apply the same restrictions to cafés, restaurants and takeaway shops as they did to Fish & Chips. The takeaway shops, in particular, were in growing competition with the friers; and the Federation did not see why what was sauce for the fried fish should not also be sauce for the fried chicken. It looks as though the Federation may get its way here—that is, if the big chains and the rival convenience foodstuffs don't launch a successful counter-lobby.

There is no reason why a modern Fish & Chip shop should smell 'offensive', apart from slovenliness and bad design. Refrigeration answers the storage problem for those which prepare their own fish, while the rangemakers have taken elaborate pains to clean up the frying process itself. There are sumps and fans and filters; infra-red lamps have turned storage boxes into sun-baths; ultra-violet and ozone have been recruited to sweeten the air. According to one theory, smells are carried in moisture, so that by passing the exhaust from the range over cold metal plates, the moisture can be condensed and only dry, odour-free air discharged. Whatever theory is right, there are now so many non-offensive shops to be found in Britain that there is no excuse for those which continue to offend.

In a sense, though, the removal of the unique restrictions on Fish & Chips, the end of its Untouchability, would mean the end of the Trade as a special caste, and its conversion into just another branch of the catering industry. Deprived of its isolation, its separateness and its character as part of the class it serves, it will surely move away from those back-street corners and take a hygienic place in the High Street, next to Boots and Smiths and Marks and Spencers. There is no reason now for a Fish & Chip shop to be any more odorous than a shoe shop or a chemist's; Derek Cooper's parody of Ramsbottom's Fish Parlour in *The Bad Food Guide* is classic but out of date. The question is, will the chip shop now be owned and operated like the chemist's and the shoe shop? Take away the smell, and any flower can be made of the same plastic.

7. Unity is Strength

ike any self-respecting club, the National Federation of Fish Friers has its own emblem—a lighthouse beaming the reassuring if tautologous motto Safety Security, its club tie ('a distinctive addition to any man's wardrobe'), its Christmas card showing a trawler making port through heavy seas, its benevolent fund, insurance discounts and Mediterranean cruises for members and their families. But a glance down the list of its 101 local associations reveals a big gap—the territory of the breakaway London and Home Counties Fish Caterers, who tend to take the *Gazette* rather than the *Review*, and who hold their meetings in the boardroom on the ground floor of the *Gazette*.

Symbol of Fraternity

Between the artisan friers of the North and the more opportunist coster-friers of London, there was an early distinction; and it was not just one of cleanliness. The distinction was accounted for partly by the shifting character of London's population, compared with the tendency to stay put around the mills and factories of the North. Fish & Chips were an offspring of the middle Industrial Revolution, and so were the working class Trade Union and Co-operative movements; all three grew up together in the North, in an atmosphere of frugal respectability, hard work and solidarity. So it is not surprising that the organization of the frying trade into associations and co-operatives began in the North of England. The first friers' co-operative of which I can find record was in Hull in 1893. The friers found themselves having to cope with 'unnecessary competition' from newcomers who insisted on setting up next to the existing shops, instead of looking for unserved areas.

We get an insight into the London frier's life about this time from a series of articles printed in *Pearson's Magazine*, in which an anonymous 'Lady Journalist' described her experiences slumming 'in different roles among the masses'—a technique still employed by some editors. The month of June 1905 took the lady to the East End of London for a day's work in a Fish & Chip shop, an apprenticeship that earned her a wage of five shillings.

She had to begin work at 4.30 a.m.; breakfast was coffee with half a cup of gin in it. Thus fortified she went to Billingsgate, where fish was being heaved about in ninety-pound trunks of ice. All kinds were mixed up together, and the middlemen or 'Bummarees' sorted it out and sold it to the fishmongers and friers who swarmed down the aisles. The fish could have been passed on to the market filleters, who would have prepared it at so much a stone, but in this case it was removed whole and cut up at the shop, which was more economical. The next job was to scrub (but not peel) the potatoes, which were then fed into a mechanical slicer. Just before noon the batter was ready and the frying began on a coal-fired range.

At noon, workmen began coming in for 'two and one'—two pennyworth of fish and one pennyworth of potatoes, the fish being in four small pieces and 'the whole making quite a good meal'. If they chose to eat on the premises, customers got a china plate and a knife and fork engraved 'Stolen from Mrs. M——'. Poor children came in for ha'pennyworth packets of 'cracklings', the bits of broken fish and crisp batter out of the baskets.

After lunch, the shop closed until the seven-to-midnight session, with the big rush between eight and ten. 'How any human being can stand the wear and tear of such a life is beyond my understanding', wrote the Lady Journalist, exhausted. But she added that the friers were respectable and thrifty and a boon to the poor. Humble and malodorous their shops might be, but they enabled many a workman's wife to fill six or eight mouths for sixpence, 'and with hot food at that, when fuel is such an expense to the poor'. The Lady Journalist noted the pre-eminence of 'children of the Ghetto' in the London Trade.

1904: Mabbott's tiled twin-pan odourless Special

There were plenty of shops in the North which would have regarded 'two and one' as an outrageous price and which continued to offer 'one and a ha'porth' as late as 1914. In spite of Chatchip's confidence that the Trade was moving up in the world, friers were always terrified that a further ha'penny increase would snap the customers' purses shut in their faces. The fact that the raw materials tended to fluctuate in price, so that there was a chance of winning back tomorrow what was lost today, often persuaded small friers to absorb long-term rising costs in their own poor standards of living. But who were they to defy the market?

In fact they were a considerable force if only they would stand together and buy, or refuse to buy, collectively. From time to time, groups of friers at the London markets would stage a boycott until prices came down. In the North, organization was more durable. In 1904 we read of 'The Fish Friers' Co-operative Association' being formed for the direct importation of Australian dripping. The *Gazette* reported that 'in Rochdale the friers have formed a very strong association which supplies everything the members require—fish, potatoes, oil, dripping, tripe, vinegar, etc., and it is in a very flourishing condition'. There was a less successful association in Leeds, and others in Lancashire; for example, Blackburn. Prior to 1907, though, there was little co-ordination between them.

Chatchip, who was always a keen Association and Federation man, maintained that the movement really became serious with the running out of the 1906 old potatoes. Instead of falling in price with the arrival of the new season's Jerseys, the remaining old potatoes soared from

70 shillings a ton to 170 shillings, making the traditional ha'porth of chips quite uneconomical. Since the friers were the main buyers of the old crop, they concluded that the dealers were deliberately exploiting them. They banded together into the Lancashire Federation of Fish Friers' Associations and either shut up their shops, tried frying new potatoes whole, or refused to fry any potatoes at all. The boycott was a success and the Lancashire men reached across the Pennines to join hands with their Yorkshire colleagues in a *United Kingdom* Federation, and it was this Federation that intervened with John Burns to stop him putting the friers behind glass screens.

But things fell apart, the centre did not hold. Not only were there regional and local rivalries and political divisions (Chatchip himself is still remembered by some as 'a red radical'); the associations were always anxious to limit entry into the Trade, arguing that too many shops meant a poor living for all. As a result, new entrants were often cold-shouldered and excluded from the organization. The arrival of successive waves of foreign friers, first Jewish, then Italian and later Cypriot, Bengali and Chinese, have always made the friers associations less inclusive than they might have been. Today, it is true, Italians are perfectly acceptable. But so they should be. They have been here two or three generations.

It was the renewed potato crisis of 1913 that woke up the organizers again. This time the *National* Federation of Fish Friers was proclaimed in Manchester, and essentially (after some purging and rejuvenation in the 1930s) it is this same body that we know today. For a genteel moment in the twenties it changed its name to the National Federation of Fish *Caterers*, 'believing that the altered times and conditions of the trade demand a more comprehensive and a better sounding titular description'. But the preciosity passed, or rather it descended to the London splinter-group (though I should add there is nothing precious about that hard-headed body of men today).

The First World War provided the new Federation with a function for which members were glad to pay their fee—badgering the Government for bigger allocations of fish, fat and potatoes, or to modify restrictions. An order had been promulgated requiring all restaurants to close by 9.30 p.m.—one of those killjoy restrictions whose main purpose is to make everyone feel better on the grounds that something has been sacrificed, however irrelevant to winning the war. The National Federation sent the second friers' deputation in history to visit Whitehall, and succeeded in winning an extra hour's opening for Fish & Chip shops, by arguing that they fed night-shifts of munitions workers.

During the 1914–18 War, the ha'penny and penn'orths became thruppenny and fourpenn'orths. In the Depression that followed, they came back to a penny and tuppence, and despite the complaints of

Chatchip did not return to a thruppenny maximum until the 1930s. The friers were kind-hearted people who lived in the midst of their customers, and though it has always been a golden rule of the Trade never to give credit, they were well aware of what a penny could mean to a child, an old-age pensioner or the wife of an unemployed miner. By efficient modern standards, the standards perhaps of a well-run chain, this was no sort of way to run a business. But it helped to keep the working class alive; and there is a sincere (if statistically unprovable) case to be made out, that during some of the worst periods in British economic history, the Fish & Chips trade has subsidized its customers and shored up their health and physique. Middle-class Southerners may poke fun, in a superior way, at the chip-munching North; but chips are a lot better than buns or bread-and-dripping, and a good deal healthier than sweets.

The Second World War restored to the Federation its task as a gadfly to the Ministry of Food. The friers complained of 'alarmingly small rations of the wrong kind of fat', of disastrous attempts to foist dried stockfish on the Trade, of blackout restrictions which deprived them of their most profitable hours of opening and made the appearance of a 'Frying Tonight' notice the tip for a queue to form. There were also complaints of weird fish-allocations which included yellow-bellied pollack, oily conger eel, and the dreaded coalie which went a dirty grey when exposed to the air (it is called 'saithe' now, and we shall all have to eat it). A well-known source of extra fat supplies was the black market outside every American airfield. But there was nothing the Federation could do to help the frier who bought half-a-hundredweight of star-spangled lard, only to find that all but the top layer was bricks.

Throughout their history, the Federation and the London group sought to improve the appearance and hygienic practices of their members. Chatchip from the very first was adamant against bare chests, braces and chewing-tobacco; a white coat he regarded as *de rigeur* from the early twenties on. Even before the First World War he was campaigning against newspaper wrapping, insisting upon an inner lining of white greaseproof. His answer to the problem of the offensive smell was to advocate more efficient frying ranges and better ventilation. This constant struggle to raise Fish & Chip shops to the level of restaurants, or at least to prevent them sliding back to that of fell-mongers and bone-boilers, occupies the leadership of the Trade to this day.

Alongside it has persisted the effort to persuade friers to be more hard-headed about their prices. What is the point of trying to be a Friend to the Poor, when you are in danger of putting yourself out of business on their behalf? And *are* the poor still with us, always? In the *Review* of March 1970 'An Average Frier' reflected: 'We have got to get rid of that thinking which used to be characteristic of most friers, that if they put up their prices to an economic level, because the poor customers "could not afford it", the frier would put himself out of business. I maintain that our customers, apart from the pensioners, are no longer so badly off . . . And even the old folks can do little better for themselves in any other establishment.'

Decimalization, acting as a kind of monetary disorientation, has certainly helped the friers round this problem. One told me: 'When I tried to put my chips up from 9d. to 10d., there was an uproar in the papers. But when they went to 5 new pence, nobody noticed!'

The Federation has a number of other problems always sizzling on its plate. It represents the Trade on several joint committees with the Fishery and Potato Industries, and it is constantly at the Government's side, plucking at the official sleeve during negotiations with Iceland or the Common Market over fishery limits. It would, I think, be prepared to raise the money for a gunboat to defend Britain's access to Icelandic waters. But it seems reconciled to the deal with the Common Market, and argues that if food prices are to go up anyway, Fish & Chips may gain some relative advantage. As for what it can do about the rising cost of the Trade's basic materials, the Federation keeps nagging the producers and is full of advice to its own members about co-operative buying schemes, wholesalers' contracts and proper cost-accounting. It still tends, though, to stand for the pure, basic Fish & Chips business, and to lean against diversifying into pies, pasties, curries, chicken, haggis, saveloys and dormice in honey.

The Federation has never cared much for 'mobiles'—Fish & Chip shops on wheels. To the settled family frier, they are the pirates and highwaymen of the Trade—ambushing his customers on the housing estate, or at the doors of the cinema, dodging rates, planning controls and hygiene regulations, and too often becoming *im*mobile and settling down as unauthorized static outlets. There have been 'mobiles' since Rouse of Oldham launched his original 'Dandy' in 1880, and complaints about them since Scotland was plagued with horse-drawn chip carts in 1908. Yet the mobile has its legitimate purposes. Its heyday was during the Second World War, when evacuees from the cities demanded their staple in the countryside; and the heyday was prolonged into the post-war years when fish, almost alone, was unrationed. Today the mobile is often the only way of getting Fish & Chips to the housebound mother and the rural housewife, and to talk as if its operator had no taxes, rates, depreciation, running costs or regulations to worry about at all is to argue somewhat too partially.

The problems of Sunday opening and foreign entrants are interlocked and have exercised Federation members a good deal of late. Nobody wants to be racist, though most friers will insist that 'customers just don't like coloured service', and they will agree that in the past the trade

1930s mobile: contented customers, unhappy friers

has recruited heavily from foreigners. But what worries the small frier nowadays is the tendency of the foreigner not to observe the Sunday closing that is one of the rules of the Trade. The Federation fights hard on this issue: 'We are trying to preserve the frier's day of leisure—his one chance to get together with his family', I was told. 'There'ld be a terrible free-for-all if a Sunday option was introduced. People who didn't want to open then, would be forced to. They'ld have to hire extra help—up would go costs—bang would go the whole family character. We're quite certain there'ld be no effective increase in sales; there'ld just be an extra day's work for the same money. From the public's point of view, it would just mean an increase in prices.' Just? But maybe the public wouldn't mind paying the extra for the convenience . . .

What has been especially worrying Federation men from Manchester to Marazion has been The Yellow Peril—the arrival of the Chinese takeaway shop. The law says that you may not sell Fish & Chips to take away from a Fish & Chip shop on a Sunday. You may eat Fish & Chips in a restaurant of any sort on a Sunday. And on a Sunday you may take away Chicken Chow Mein—and Chips, if you are that sort of person. And what about taking away Fish & Chips from a Chicken Chow Mein shop on a Sunday? That, apparently, is all right. The shop is not, or says it is not, a Fish & Chip shop. But it *is*, it *is*! cry the friers indignantly.

Meanwhile the outer defences of Sabbatarianism are crumbling. At many seaside resorts, Sunday closing is observed only when the holiday-makers have gone home. 'What d'you think we want them here for—to learn to use chopsticks?' asked one seaside frier indignantly. And another wondered suspiciously whether all those Chinese he saw helping in the shop round the corner were really members of the same family. 'You can't tell, can you?' he demanded, 'And if they're just employees, are they on the legal wages and hours, like everybody else's? That's what I'd like to know. Working like blacks, they are . . .'

The Chinese—some from Malaysia, some from Hong Kong—

continue their frying cheerfully and inscrutably. They are excellent fish cooks, though inclined towards inflated batter, and they will even, if the barbarous British devils demand it, stoop to selling them rice and chips with a dollop of bilious green curry-sauce. To everyone's surprise, the market seems to have absorbed them after all, and the more far-sighted British friers think the threat of a great leap forward into their business is a thing of the past. I suspect, myself, that the dropout rate from this gruelling trade leaves room for more newcomers than the native friers care to admit. The Federation has put out literature in Chinese, as well as Greek, but fears that the foreigners do not fully appreciate what the N.F.F.F. has to offer.

The fact is, however, that while the Federation claims 'the bigger type of frier' as its member, and may well have a majority of the Trade in terms of volume, it only represents some 6,000 of Britain's 14,000 or so friers. And there is, inevitably, another side to its case. One big London frier described the Federation to me as 'Luddites'. He went on: 'What they're really afraid of, with their Sunday closing and their planning controls, is someone *good* opening up near their shops. Sunday closing is crazy—that's when everyone *wants* to buy, and would buy *more*. The Fried Chicken and Hamburger people open on Sunday; *we* can't because of this mediæval law. There's tremendous lobbying to keep it—the Federation have got at least two M.P.s briefed on their side —but the consumer's best interest will be served by opening up. I can promise you there'll be something in the works soon to make sure we can.'

Over the Federation's dead body. It last defeated Sunday Opening at its conference of 1970, and by a handsome margin. The Federation is essentially a commonwealth of local associations, with its elder statesmen, its 'character' and its perennial rebels. Every spring, some two hundred delegates and wives meet at some seaside resort like Scarborough or Tynemouth or Southampton. Opening the proceedings, the mayor tells funny stories about Fish & Chips and newspaper, and then reminds his audience that (as they know full well) it is no laughing matter. Indeed, their a-*peel* is the very *backbone* of the Englishman's diet (*applause*—except from the Scottish and Welsh delegates). There is a Presidential Banquet and Ball (long dresses and dinner-jackets), with a toast proposed by somebody from the Potato Board or the White Fish Authority, then a raffle for two dozen boxes of frozen chips presented by the manufacturer, and the presentation of the Golf, Putting and Bowls trophies. There may also be a fashion parade or hat-show for the ladies.

At the 1971 conference there was some feeling that a little too much time was being spent on fun and games, and despite protests on behalf of the ladies, a resolution was carried that in future Conference should not adjourn to play bowls, and that the whole second day out of the three should be devoted solely to business.

Event	No. of Tickets Required	Price per Ticket	Cost £ p
Monday, after conference. Ladies' Putting Competition for the Ross Group Silver Rose Bowl at the Arnold Palmer Putting Green.		Free	
Monday, 9 pm. Civic reception by the Mayor of Tynemouth at the Park Hotel.		Free	
Tuesday, 2 pm. Ladies' outing to Otterburn Mill. Tea to be taken at Otterburn Tower (inclusive).		75p	
Tuesday, after conference. Bowls Tournament for the Melhuish Crispex Cup at the Tynemouth Bowling Club.		Free	
Wednesday, 2 pm. Golf tournament for the S. H. Phillips Goldensheaf Trophy at Tynemouth Golf Club.		50p	
Wednesday, President's Banquet and Ball at the Park Hotel.*		£2.50	
		Total..	

1972 Friers' Conference sideshows: book now

In 1971 business ranged from the problems of joining the E.E.C., and of Town Planning, the price of oil, a 'chipping grade' for potatoes, what to do with unwanted chicken giblets, misleading publicity about fish prices, and whether to limit the President of the Federation to no more than five consecutive terms in office. And the call went forth from President Arnold Scholes (as it had done for the past six years): 'Every frier will be richer for joining the Federation. I urge you all to carry this message to every non-member. Face the future with confidence, with the National Federation of Fish Friers.'

But confidence in what? A year later, the grumbles about the grading, quality and price of the British Potato had risen to a roar; and in Parliament, the friers' interests suffered one of their nastiest setbacks since the days of the Offensive Trade. The Commons voted 217 to 200 against exempting Fish & Chips and other small catering establishments from the dreaded Common Market Value Added Tax. In the jargon, what had been sought was 'zero-rating'. In vain, from the Labour Front Bench Mr. Joel Barnett painted a harrowing picture of millions forced on to the streets, Fish & Chips in hand. For the Government, Mr. John Nott (of St. Ives and the Treasury) sternly ruled that 'if fish and chips are consumed on the premises, then they are liable to VAT; but if they are taken away they are not liable to VAT . . . If the Honourable Member wishes to eat fish and chips in a car park, then it will not be taxable.' Mr. Nott ventured to forecast that this would go down in the annals of Westminster as The Fish and Chips Debate; but there were also problems arising out of winkles, jellied eels, haggis and pies. Sir Gerald Nabarro (Conservative, Worcs., S.): '. . . and Worcester sauce.'

8. Home on the Range

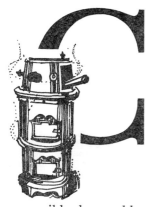

Chatchip describes an old-time fish frier, as if he were the demon cook in *Titus Groan*:

'He used to manipulate the fires with a long-handled shovel and to all appearances gave one the impression he was firing up a factory boiler. While the great panful of chipped potatoes was being cooked he would, in the intervals between "firing up" and "stirring up" the contents of the pan, stand behind the counter with his greasy hands in his pockets, chewing away at a great quid of tobacco. These operations successfully accomplished with as much splash and splutter as possible, he would advance to the counter and in stentorious tones ring out: "Come on, in your thousands! We are the people who feed the hungry! Come on penn'orths; stand back ha-porths!"'

Some of that comes under the heading Tones We Doubt Ever Rang Out, but bearing in mind that a fair number of friers were in fact retired stokers, the impression in general is a fair one.

Once the chipped potato had joined the fish and deep frying became the rule for both partners, it was logical for the friers to equip themselves with the sort of ranges already being built for the tripe-dressers, soap-boilers and fat-renderers. Some readers will remember the old coppers once used for boiling sheets: a deep cauldron fitted into the top of a large brick box, with a coal fire in a grate underneath and a flue at the back. A two-cauldron version of this, one for the Fish and the other for the Chips, launched the Trade on its way and lasted, in principle, for almost a century in some cases. A great many refinements were introduced—glazed bricks, internal ducts, draught controls and insulation—but one firm of rangemakers tells me that up to five years ago it knew of three of its pre-1914 ranges still in action, modelled on this pattern. And I have seen reports of coal or coke ranges being taken out of service in London in 1962 and in Batley and Sheffield as recently as 1970. The

1900-ish. Engineer-designed and portable

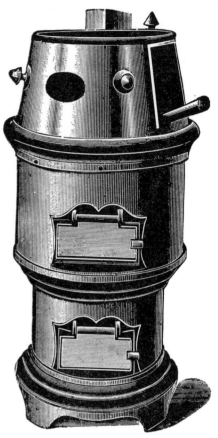

Batley frier, reluctantly yielding to progress, declared there was no finer way of frying fish; it gave them 'an individual flavour'. Joe Lees of Mossley, looking back to the early 1900s, agreed, saying: 'Jack Rouse built us one with tiled brick, twenty pounds the lot. Those old ranges had iron pans weighing sixty or seventy pounds. That's why I think Fish & Chips were better than they are today . . .'

Certainly the heavy iron pans must have resisted the sudden loss of heat caused by the dumping of a big load into the fat. But they must also have been hard to warm up quickly, and very inflexible in use. The fact that they were fired by coal added to the dirt in the shop and the storage space required, and made it difficult for a woman to manage the shop alone. In the early days, frying was a man's work, and the type of man who took to it was not always fussy about the congealed fat and batter that soaked into the brickwork and built up into a layer of thick linoleum on top. The stench as the range heated up for a day's frying was appalling.

The pans were some eighteen inches deep and held several gallons of oil or dripping. Loose lids to stop the fat splashing were available quite early on, followed by the controversial hoods and the flues to convey the fumes away. However, as Dr. Ballard pointed out in his report of 1876, the pans were frequently opened for 'manipulation', while the bad design of many hoods and the fluctuating draughts in the shops as people entered and left, made these improvements less impressive in practice than they were in appearance.

The next improvement, however, was to fit a cast iron sheet or slab on to the top of the range, which could then easily be kept clean. A disadvantage of the brick range was that, being a fixture, it became the property of the landlord if the frier had to move. It was a bulky object, requiring strong foundations, and this, too, was a disadvantage when so many friers wanted to operate out of a back shed or a front parlour. Thus two kinds of 'portable', or at least transportable ranges were developed. The first, essentially a chip-frier, was a cylindrical affair with the fire under a single pan and a stove-pipe coming out of the back. But this, although it became popular for use in carts or at fairgrounds, limited the scale of operations. Hence the full-scale portable was developed.

Late Edwardian: unlovely, but effective

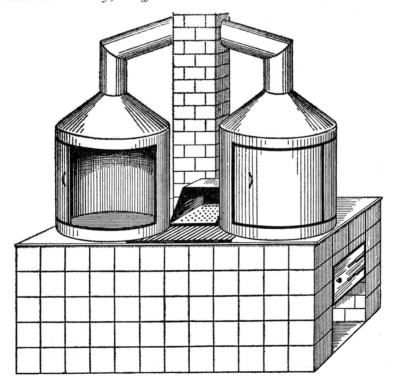

I should explain here that all early ranges were 'wall ranges', sited against the wall like a fireplace, so that the smoke went directly up the chimney, and the frier stood with his back to the customers. Later, with forced draughts, two other types became possible: the 'counter range', where the range is part of the counter, and the frier serves over the top of it or round the side; and the 'island range', which stands behind the counter with friers working at the back of it and pushing the orders through to servers at the front—a design which implies a pretty large-scale operation.

Mr. Teuten (who later went into partnership with a Mr. Robottom, to produce the well-known Wizard range) set up his range-making business near Billingsgate in 1869. A rather similar business had been started by Nuttalls of Rochdale a few years earlier, while Acme of Leeds and Faulkners of Oldham claim to go back to the decade of the 1870s. Clearly the small foundry or sheet-metal works could pick up all kinds of odd jobs, as successor to the blacksmith of earlier times, and among them were orders from the bakers, boilers and friers who made up the catering industry. It is really impossible to say who made the first Fish & Chip range as such.

Faulkners (the family were originally hatters) believe that the ranges they supplied in the 1870s were almost invariably used for chips only—often to be sold with tripe. And the same is true of Rouse's celebrated 'Dandy'. Working in a cellar in Oldham, young John Rouse fitted a hand-pulled chipper and a single-pan frier into a sturdy hand-cart. With a canopy over the working end and a tall chimney at the other, it looked like a concertinaed version of Stephenson's *Rocket*. As the legend tells, Rouse wheeled it through the streets of Oldham one September evening in 1880, giving away his 'Hot Chip Potatoes' for nothing; and within three days 'the demand for hot chips was to spread like wildfire through Lancashire'. In fact it had spread, and was being fed (if less picturesquely) long before. What Rouse did was to make the Trade mobile and establish his company, as it remains, one of the leaders in its field—a pioneer, for example, of the electric range.

One of the earliest big advertisers of equipment was Mabbott, of Phoenix Ironworks, Manchester. One of this company's announcements, in 1904, made much of its development of the mobile or 'Shop on Wheels', of which three hundred had already been built. 'With one of these vans,' explained Mabbott, confirming the worst fears of a later generation of friers, 'the shopkeeper goes to his customers; he does not wait until they come to him. He pays no rent, rates or taxes. Many have built up a business something like the milk business, only the customer expects the van every evening about supper-time; while in the daytime the "Shop on Wheels" is to be found at the entrance of some large works or colliery. Saturday afternoon finds him at the football match, and where fish and chips are not appropriate, these vans carry coffee and buns. They are to be seen in the streets of London, serving light refreshments to the coachmen and footmen who have to stand outside various mansions where receptions are held.' It conjures up an aromatic picture of Embassy Row in 1904. But the horse-drawn chip shop had a long life. In 1920, Acme were still marketing a two-pan model with a roguishly gipsy appearance.

Mabbott's mobile of 1904: just the job for the Embassy mob

But while the new mobiles were relatively airy and efficient in design, the durable old brick ranges were steadily dragging down the friers into the category of 'offensive trade'. Chatchip quite rightly agitated for 'up-to-date ranges, closed pans and through draughts', and when there were objections to the steam being discharged outside the shop, he retorted: 'Rising steam cannot be any annoyance to anybody except balloonists and aviators, and they are at present a negligible quantity.'

As the Trade attracted increasing attention from the public health inspectors, it occurred to rangemakers that the answer to the smell problem might be to feed the fumes back into the range itself, through an intricate maze of ducts and channels. There were the complications of soot and clots of grease collecting, and a somewhat greater risk of fire to the slovenly frier who omitted to scrape out regularly, but there might also be greater heat-efficiency. Acme claimed they had invented an odour-free range by 'passing all vapours through the fires, thus cremating them'. That was in 1900. According to Faulkner, it was in 1899 that a Glamorganshire frier named George Rye sent *them* designs for a range incorporating not only anti-splash trays and pan-covers, but also conduits 'for removing the steam and effluvia'. Even in 1888, there was a report of a range in Greenwich which 'consumed its own smoke and steam', so once again it seems impossible to award an unchallengeable first prize.

By 1914 the portable range was becoming generally accepted. Sometimes it was a cast-iron monster with brass fittings that left black marks on the frier's apron, but increasingly it was based upon an iron frame into which the pans, ducts and grate or burners were fitted, and the whole clad in tiles or enamel. It began to dawn upon the frier that, at the same time, he might improve his image by making his range a thing of beauty. Mirrors, mosaics and Dutch tiles appeared, and Acme marketed a splendid model with fitted aspidistra-holders. Few aspidistras can have survived the climate up there for long.

Coal or coke continued to be the standard fuel for Fish & Chip shops until the 1920s. Chatchip held out against the detested gas until 1925. With the 1930s, however, gas swept all before it; it was clean, flexible and required no storage space. Electricity, although even cleaner, was handicapped (as it continues to be) by the assumption of high running costs; it advanced little beyond the experimental stage before the 1950s. Oil (which meant paraffin until recently) was almost universally rejected, and even now makers like Bateman feel obliged to make a special case for it. Like oil-fired central heating, upon which it is based, it is a case in which relatively clumsy gear and expensive installation and storage have to be balanced against appreciably lower running costs. In general, though, the victory still rests with gas; notwithstanding some grumbles about the new-fangled stuff from the North Sea.

Frying is only the climax of the frier's business. Before long, thought was being given to mechanizing the tedious preparation of the potatoes. Londoners remained primitives into the twentieth century, but it became common practice in the nineteenth-century Lancashire chip shops to dump the potatoes into a barrel, throw in some pieces of broken brick, and stir the lot with a broom handle until a proportion of the skin had been scoured off.

The first advance upon this was the use of a 'peggy stick' or 'dolly'—
a kind of five-legged stool with a long handle, originally made for churn-

Owen's Original potato-scraping Dolly

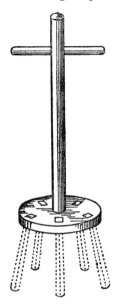

ing tubs of laundry. (I saw a couple in a Belsize Park antique shop
lately, so they may not have been confined to the North.) A Lancashire
frier named Owen refined this still further by covering the legs of the
'peggy' with the type of abrasive material used for nutmeg graters. The
process of grinding the skins off was strenuous, but if kept up long
enough, surprisingly thorough. A Sheffield frier produced Collins
Patent Potato Peeler, a kind of minature lathe which rotated the potato
against a cutter, removing a continuous spiral of peel from end to end.
It took time, but I saw the device still being demonstrated effectively at
a London 'Ideal Home' Exhibition only a few years ago.

During the 1870s the Wonder Potato Peeler—a drum lined with

Collins' potato-lathe. South Yorkshire

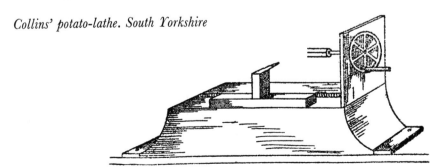

gritty material—appeared, but it had no gears and since it took a load of thirty pounds of potatoes, it was hard work spinning it. 1885 saw the smoother 'Rumbler' on the scene, an abrasive drum that rotated while lying horizontally in a trough of water. The operator had to wear an oilskin and clogs so as not to get soaked, but the Rumbler was the classic peeler for almost forty years, and in the early 1900s it was brought up to date when Robinson of Manchester introduced a small gas engine to turn the barrel.

Hand-pulled chippers, which squeezed the potatoes one by one through a grid of knives, came in during the 1870s and have remained a valued standby ever since. The modern electrically driven chipper which slices the potato one way, then slides it over and slices it the other, is a good deal faster, but subject to mechanical failures. Together with an electrical peeler, it can bring the cost of preparation machinery up to £200.

With the number of frying shops ranging between 14,000 and 30,000 over the past seventy years, the Fish & Chips Trade has meant a steady living for up to a score of small, specialized firms of rangemakers. It says a lot for the slow, loyal, conservative character of the indsutry, its devotion to known families and traditions, that they have still not been rationalized like the motor-car or aircraft industries into a mere handful. With the exception of Preston and Thomas in Cardiff and Bateman near Birmingham, the location of these firms clearly reflects the roots and origins of the Trade. They are concentrated along an axis that runs Manchester (one firm), Oldham (four firms), Rochdale (two firms), Huddersfield (one firm), Halifax (two firms), and Leeds (six firms), all within fifty miles of each other.

Far be it from me to recommend or advertise one above the others. I cannot resist noting, though, a few names and features that pluck at the layman's eye. For example, the consistent sexiness of Frank Ford's range of ranges—a blonde, busty style that can be traced from the electric model of 1932 to the fashionable Concorde of the seventies. Ford's glamour has only been matched by Bateman's Carousel, a vast horseshoe-shaped console whose 552 square-inch trapezoidal pan was proclaimed 'the breakthrough of the century'; fine for serving vast throngs, it was agreed, but a bit pricey. There is our old friend Acme, pioneers of the export market, who have dispatched to the Soviet Union a mammoth range with fish going through on a conveyor belt, untouched by hand. There is Procter, who claim to have sold a range to an Eskimo, who build 'up to a standard—not down to a price', and whose Earl incorporates Twin Ducting. There is Portland, with the Solar 70 counter range with Simmerstat controlled infra-red heaters; Hopkins ('Not just a pretty face—More like Perfection, actually') who announce sternly 'No high-pressure salesmen—it's up to you to contact us';

The frier in action: Mr. F. Stratis at Myddleton Quality Fish Bar, Bowes Park, London

The good frier eats his own wares: Mr. Stratis at lunch

Mallinson, whose Vista Mark II offers cool frontage and vivid display; Robinson, of whose Excel it is said that the axe-head gas jet packs more power than any of its rivals; and my special favourites, Triumph-Scarbron, whose ranges comply with the exacting standards of the National Sanitation Foundation of America. No Paris Spring Fashion Parade or International Motor Show is more *à la mode* than these.

Running one's eye through the catalogues over the years, one notices the trend of fashion in rangemaking. In the 1920s, designs were like sideboards or upright pianos, and there was much tile-work. In the 1930s, pictures flourished on backplates, chrome and the cinema-foyer crept in, designs became more severe. With the post-war revival came the counter models (first introduced in 1936) with electric fans drawing the fumes away under the floor. But superficially, the 1930-ish look continued until 1948, when infra-red heating of storage boxes came in. The sharp-edged, stainless steel look took over, and 1960 found a proliferation of mechanical frills, with knobs and dials lending a computer look to what had once been just a great big cooker. A glance through the styles of the early seventies shows formica advancing, the steely look losing ground, and *feet* (once hidden behind skirtings) peeping out once more.

A three-pan wall range for a suburban shop can now set you back about £1,500, though with pan replacements it can last you between twenty and forty years. You would probably buy it through a finance company or bank, putting one-third down and paying the rest over two years. The pans are thermostatically controlled so as not to overheat the oil; but if you are sensible you will order something with a built-in automatic fire-extinguisher. Fire remains the plague of the frier.

A visit to a rangemaker's works produces an eerie sensation of living in two centuries at once. There are the ranges themselves, space-age and gleaming, and there are the long-haired apprentices tuning in rock music on their transistors. But there, too, is the workshop itself, looking like the birthplace of some very early flying machine, and white-haired craftsmen forming the stainless steel as if they were Renaissance silver-smiths. 'A very highly skilled trade,' I was told, 'It's all hand-formed; can't be pressed; have to do it by mallets over a stake.'

Almost every range is tailor-made to the customer's order—nothing on spec. With forty-five production workers, and about three weeks to complete each model, the weekly output might be no more than two or three. The cautious economics of the average rangemaker prefer it this way. Most British manufacturers have heard the siren voices from across the Atlantic, urging them to expand beyond their wildest dreams and ship ranges by the hundred to the American market. But while several have done business there, and some (like Triumph) have gone to great pains to meet the stringent American regulations banning solder,

1920s range design: gas–coke–electric

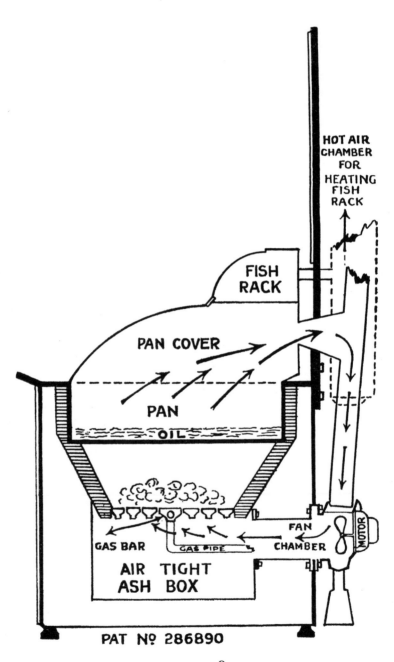

HOT AIR
CHAMBER
FOR
HEATING
FISH
RACK

FISH
RACK

PAN COVER

PAN

OIL

FAN
CHAMBER

MOTOR

GAS BAR

GAS PIPE

AIR TIGHT
ASH BOX

PAT Nº 286890

98

hollow feet and hard-to-clean angles, all have come to the conclusion
that the United States Fish & Chips craze is a flash in the pan that can
only burn the rangemaker who plays with it.

'There's millions and millions of pounds waiting over there,' one of
them told me wistfully, 'they're making two thousand pounds a week
out of a single range in Denver. But I don't trust it—it won't last. They
go through these crazes out there. Fish & Chips aren't a tradition, you
see, like they are here . . .'

9. Fry, Lechery, Fry

Shakespeare

n fact, the libertine finds very little scope in a Fish & Chip shop. 'It ruins your evenings, there's the counter between you and the birds, and (*don't* let's face it) there's even less sex-appeal to frying fish than there is to driving a bus.' And since frying hours generally coincide with the open hours of public houses, it is not much of a job for the drinking man, either. Add their resistance to doing business on Sundays, and the friers have good grounds for regarding themselves as among the most respectable members of the community. There are those who accuse them of financial sleight-of-hand, and claim that there are more Jensens and Scimitars parked behind Fish & Chip shops than the friers' tax returns could explain; but the Trade also includes a generous proportion of economic innocents and workers-for-next-to-nothing who are virtually giving their services away.

In 1911 the *Gazette* published the accounts of 'A Successful Fish Frier'. Success to him meant that with a turnover of £10 a week he was clearing a profit of about £3.30 p. (say £163 a year). One must allow for the declining value of money; but today, in a list of businesses for sale in the Home Counties, you may find weekly turnovers of between £300 and £450 a week, and higher. A Greek frier in North London defined happiness to me as clearing £30 a week. But I have also seen the audited accounts of a frier in the South-West whose net profit was £7,000 from a turnover of £27,000 a year. The Trade today ranges from the three per cent of shops which belong to chains of two or more, to the vast majority of independent family businesses with a couple of part-time and a couple of full-time employees. It is at the width of this range that I want to look now.

Harry Ramsden's, at White Cross, between Leeds and Ilkley, is no small family fish shop. It employs 150 people in shifts, and the car park would take a race meeting. Working there behind the pans, you might start at £25 a week and rise to £35 if you put in fifty-four hours. The main occupational disease is sheer exhaustion. Publicity and a fortunate location at a busy roundabout have helped towards making Ramsden's the Mecca of North Country coach tours. The people shuffle in and out of it from 11.30 a.m. to 11.30 p.m., as if they were going to see the panda at the Zoo. You can either go to the takeaway side and eat on the rows of benches out in front, or sit inside in the bright, bustling restaurant with chandeliers from the ceiling, damask on the walls and soft carpet underfoot. You may have to queue for a quarter of an hour to get in, but your stay will average thirty-seven minutes from sit-down to pay-up.

I must confess I have heard criticism of the product on the takeaway side. But then, in my own heretical view, it is a mistake to carry out Fish & Chips in any case. To quote the patriarch Joe Lees: 'You should have it in an open paper and eat it straight away'. So, substituting plate for paper, I prefer to judge Ramsden's by its inside service, which is West Riding cuisine at its best. My special haddock with chips, tea, bread and butter cost 41p.—which, on the face of it, is more than in Central London; but the fish was incomparably more plump, hot and succulent, the batter crisp and thin, not inflated or tough, and the chips—just *so*. I was appalled to see, at the next table, coffee being served ready mixed with milk in the brutish Australian manner.

The original Harry Ramsden is no more. He was to Yorkshire Fish & Chips what Colonel Sanders is to Kentucky Fried Chicken, as improbable as a real Santa Claus, a mixture of showman and businessman. His gimmicks ranged from celebrating forty years in the Trade by reinstating 'penn'orths and ha'porths' for a day, to infiltrating a bogus winner into the annual road-walk race, with an advertisement for Ramsden's on his back.

Harry started in a still-preserved hut at Guiseley tram terminus, not far from the existing restaurant. He moved into solid premises in 1928, and sold out to the no less talented Eddie Stokes in 1954. Today, Ramsden's belongs to Associated Fisheries, which means the Seafarer chain, but the takeover has been a discreet one and the old image is being enhanced rather than replaced. Seafarer public relations men talk mystically about Harry Ramsden's secret batter recipe.*

With one-and-a-half million customers a year and a turnover of about £300,000, the contemplation of Ramsden's is conducive to hysteria. 'A particularly gruelling sort of existence,' says Wilfred Bush, the man-

* *Since my visit, there have been further upheavals : a new front, new kitchens, and Wilfred Bush has left to run a rival house. But Ramsden's restaurant and atmosphere remain.*

ager. 'The real essence is keeping the staff in the right frame of mind. If we're going to have Fish & Chips, let's get it right.' In other words, let's concentrate on the well-loved and perfected product and not muck about with chicken or curry or steak.

Bush has a background of business administration and the West Country rather than shirt-sleeved frying in the North, but his command of the subject is by now comprehensive. His statistics are specially terrifying. In one year, Ramsden's used:

173	tons of fish
380	tons of potatoes
28	tons of flour
68	tons of dripping
1	ton of salt
1,100	gallons of vinegar
6,750	tins of baked beans
5,000	tins of processed peas
5	miles of bread
$5\frac{3}{4}$	tons of butter
80,000	cartons of ice-cream
800	boxes of chocolate biscuits
8,000	tins of soup
89,000	bottles of soft drinks
2,000	tins of orange juice
800	tins of tomato juice
18,000	bottles of tomato sauce
4,500	bottles of H.P. sauce
$\frac{3}{4}$	ton of coffee
$2\frac{1}{2}$	tons of tea
10,000	gallons of milk
	and
$6\frac{1}{2}$	tons of sugar for the sugar-bowls.

Plaice : most popular flatfish

Plaice and halibut are on the menu, too, but the staple—80 per cent —is haddock. That's how it has to be in the West Riding, and it must be fried in dripping as well. The fish comes from Grimsby, fresh, wet fillets in huge tins for the restaurant: 'We skin it, cut out our Special across the shoulders and get two or three ordinary pieces from the rest'. But the takeaway shop now has to use frozen Faero portions: 'We had no choice; fresh haddock is getting so scarce and desperate, it's becoming a luxury. People in Yorkshire don't want to know about cod, but they'll have to soon.' The Faero portions tend to dry up if kept hanging about for long, but if treated right they are more consistent than the fresh. The pieces are dipped in batter and laid in the pan by hand: 'Just you try *using* those hygienic tongs.' They take from five to eight minutes to cook, and you could be watching fifty items in a pan three feet by two.

The potatoes come from Lincolnshire at £18·20p. a ton. But in May and June, between the main crops when new potatoes are no good for chipping, Ramsden's have to use Cyprus potatoes, which are excellent but cost up to £55 a ton. 'Swings and roundabouts—averages out over the year,' says Bush.

They fry at about 375 degrees Fahrenheit. Much under that, and the chips get soggy. But beef dripping has a lower flashpoint than oil. It starts to break down at 400 degrees, and catches fire around 450, so you haven't a lot of margin. If it does overheat, a bell rings and somebody does something with foam, carbon dioxide and asbestos blankets. As for the legendary batter: 'Plain flour and water plus our own secret powder, beaten with an antiquated mixer; it's like a doctor's prescription, though.' Could the secret be baking powder? 'Sort of . . .'

The great batter mystery—or myth—is the point upon which every frier, however small, feels that *he* is right and everyone else wrong. 'However successful the frier may be in preparation or frying, this will avail him little if he cannot produce good batter,' says Reeves' *Modern Fish Frier*. He goes on into a depressing exposition of how you may have to blend several different flours to match your local water, how the mixture should ferment to a certain degree, how it becomes loose and flakey if kept too long, leathery if used too soon, and how the entire batch can be ruined by the weather.

It is agreed, even today, that there must be aeration of the batter, but the debate rages whether to achieve this mechanically (by whisking), chemically (with baking powders), or biologically (by adding yeast). There are as many versions as there are cures for the hiccoughs.

'I've tried mixing in a bottle of Guinness, using yeast, adding lemon juice, beating in eggs, but I've always come back to good, plain flour', says my own favourite frier: 'I take three pints of water to four pounds of flour—I use water that's been left to run—add a little bicarbonate of soda and mix it with a wooden spoon to a thick, creamy paste. Then let it stand for half an hour. Mix a new lot for each session, and thin it down in the counter-bowl as you use it. Some people add the bottom of last session's batter to the next session's, but that's mumbo-jumbo . . .'

Batter can also mean hanky-panky. A thick stodgy batter will make the portion seem heavier, but it will take longer to cook and be doughy inside. A puffy batter will make it look bigger, but there is apt to be dis-illusion when the customer penetrates the cocoon and finds a mere sliver of fish inside. A watery mixture will explode when it hits the fat, leaving the fish naked and filling the pan with splinters of batter. One should sieve the pan to remove the larger fragments, and dump in a load of chips to deal with the curse of the dreaded black specks. Scraps are put into a special container to drain off the oil in them; they can actually be sold to a contractor for about 10p. a stone. What he does with them is his secret.

The simple, if cheating, answer to the agonizing problems of batter-ology is to buy a ready-mixed brand and follow the instructions on the packet. A detail for attention here is that frozen portions of fish (of which more in a moment) have to be cooked while they are solid. Otherwise the crystals that form on the surface will vaporize and blow holes in your batter. One therefore needs to buy a special frozen-portions mixture. One also needs to make sure that the oil or fat is at the proper tempera-ture (somewhere between 360 and 380 degrees on your thermostat) and that the fish is slid into the pan delicately. The immortal Chatchip insisted that it should be laid in with the skin side *under,* so that it con-tracted and 'plumped the fish up'. But there's very little skin about these days (except on plaice) and I think the flavour suffers. My own con-sultant, by the way, puts his newest fat in the right-hand pan, partly used fat in the middle one, and his oldest batch in the left-hand pan for chips only. He's a dripping man, as they tend to be in the West and in Yorkshire, and every morning he cuts the fat out of the pans in solid blocks and shaves the sediment off the bottom, which you can't do with oil.

Spotted dogfish (alias rock salmon); man-eaten not man-eater

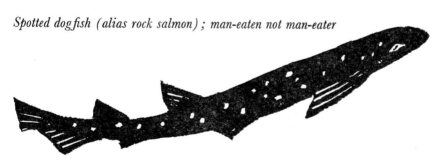

As to what fish you might be frying, that is largely a matter of where you are doing business; though fashions have been changed by short-ages. Cheshire, Lancashire, South Wales and the West used to be hake country, but the Spaniards wiped that out. Now they have switched to cod. Yorkshire is for haddock, of course, but down in London they will eat anything that swims—cod, haddock, plaice, skate and 'rock' (which means dogfish). Up in Scotland they fancy small haddock. Halibut is the top-price delicacy far and wide, unless you count scampi and, in some places, Dover sole, salmon and trout (which would cost you 50p. or more). Ah! If Chatchip could hear them now, calling for 'trout and five-penceworth' down in Pisces on the Finchley Road, he would know the Trade had finally made it to the heights. But I doubt whether he would approve of the chicken, curry and chop suey.

Herring and mackerel are not friers' fish because, being oily, they ruin the stock in the pan. But in the far west of Cornwall you get delicious fries of pouting and ling and megrim—unbelievably cheap, but I shall not tell you where.

Besides coming 'fresh', defrosted, or in blocks still to be defrosted, fish now arrives at the frier's in laminated blocks, to be cut up with an electric saw; or in ready-shaped frozen portions which go straight into the pan. This may astonish the housewife who is used to cooking her fish when it is thawed and flabby. There are two points here: first, that the far greater heat of the deep oil enables the frier to cook quite differently, sealing the outside and turning the moisture inside into steam. Fried fish is really *steamed fish*, with a crust round it, and the art is in the balanced cooking of the two. Second, the thawing of fish is bound to involve the bleeding away of its juices, a degree of drying, so that if it is plunged into the oil *un*thawed that loss will be minimal and succulence be preserved. There are friers who rebut this; but there are also customers who *like* their fish dry.

The real advantage of the prepared frozen portion is that since each is identical with the next, the frier knows exactly what he is getting and what he is giving for the money, and he can adjust his price against his cost accordingly. The unappetizing term for this is 'portion control', meaning there is no risk of anyone getting that little bit extra which is one of life's unexpected pleasures. To the old-fashioned frier the frozen portion is an affront to his skill with the knife, and even to modernists it lacks the human touch of spontaneous home-cooking. 'The customers look at those dreary squares and triangles, think of fish fingers, and buzz straight out of the door', said one.

Even chips can be bought by the plastic sack or frozen boxfull. Why not stop doing your own? Because to most friers, who have already invested in a peeler and a chipper, it would be yet another step away from the traditional Trade and into the anonymous Fast Food Industry. Most friers have still to be convinced of the economics. Depending on the method of peeling used (and the maintenance and efficiency of the machinery), a ton of evenly graded potatoes should yield around three-quarters of a ton of raw chips, which will make half a ton cooked. But the prepared chip has to bear the added cost of preservation and pack-aging, above what it may save, and there are still Old English doubts about unnaturalness and additives. 'Up to now we've been the last really honest, unadulterated meal on the market. If we're not careful, we'll be feeding the public reconstituted chips and fish-type woven soya-pulp, and saying "it's all for your *convenience*". I hate that word "*convenience*".' The speaker was in his thirties, a Midlands man.

Certainly there are many friers whom it is hard to imagine doing anything for convenience, or even for sound business reasons. Friers tend to be uncommunicative, even secretive, about the profit and loss side of their work; and one is driven to the conclusion that a fair pro-portion don't really know what they are doing in business terms, and don't care either. Sometimes the shop is run as a kind of hobby; or the owner feels it is a step up socially to have his own business, even if it is paying him less well than wage-earning. The hours, though they can be long, are not rigidly prescribed. One can always hang up a 'closed today' sign and go for a picnic, or shut down for a week or two altogether at holiday time. In Cornwall, about a third of the National Federation members close down for the winter. Compared with pub-keeping, baking or grocering, Fish & Chips can be startlingly unbusinesslike.

How, then, should the small frier join the race set by Harry Rams-den's stride forward into the twenty-first century? He might, for a start, consult Charles Rogers, designer for the White Fish Authority's Shop Improvement Service, and ask him to give the old shop a face-lift. For the past six years, Rogers has been roaming the land, doing 30,000 miles and a hundred designs a year for friers who want his services, for a very modest fee. His designs stress neatness, brightness, cleanness, in the modern manner: blue and white and a touch of formica-woodwork. He prefers to *allude* to fish rather than wave them about. Fish murals, fish tiles and the tanks of live fish so often suggested to him are played down as 'too cannibalistic'. Most friers, when they can bring themselves to articulate their ideas at all, ask if he can 'get more in', especially more people. Often they have to be told there is too much in already, for there should be at least as much space behind the counter in a small shop as there is in front. Rogers is seldom told the results of his services, and sometimes he has to drive past the shop months later to find our whether the design has been carried out at all. Where it has, he thinks trade goes up by from 20–40 per cent—although the frier wouldn't want the tax man to jump to conclusions, and usually complains about how much it has all cost.

I once asked an American caterer what he thought of our Fish & Chip shops. 'I don't really think it's a business at all,' he said, 'it appears to be some kind of a way of life . . .'

Personally, I am not sure that only applies to our Fish & Chips.

10. Wider Still and Wider

bu Dhabi looks like a city whose population has not yet been delivered. Its low horizon and wide open streets would drive the M.G.B. and Porsche crowd to distraction, but there is not a sports car to be seen. There are people somewhere, but under the sun-bleached skies of the Gulf, they take refuge, and only come out at night. Inside the Hotel, the management fights a running battle to keep the gentlemen wearing their ties, though sheikhs in robes are exempt. One Englishman approaches another in the lobby: 'Excuse me, are you Babcock and Wilcox?' Neither. Venturing recklessly into the open, one stumbles off a tessellated pavement into a sand-drift, totters over deep trenches on splintering gang-planks. Behind the show-case shops—the German chemist's, full of Hindus discreetly requesting 'something for weakness' —are the inevitable Indian snackeries, the Malabar Merchants and Freddie's Just-Fit Jackets, all loyally displaying the ruler's portrait in the window.

The Golden Fish Snack Bar—*Al-Samakeh Al-Thahabiya*—is a cut above all that. It is situated on the sterile Corniche, or sea front, at the foot of a block of flats, cunningly sited between two colonies of expatriate oil company employees. The exterior should meet all Charles Rogers' demands for neatness and cleanliness, though the interior decor is a night-clubby red and blue, with red curtains, and there is Rock Musak coming through the ceiling. It is essentially a sit-down establishment, which always means the price is going to be higher, and this being the Gulf where even the population is largely imported, prices are higher still. The fish is locally caught *hammour*, but the potatoes, like the proprietor, come from Lebanon. A plate of Fish & Chips costs you the equivalent of 50p. *Hammour* is a thick, heavy beast, and they serve it cut into fingers, egg-and-breadcrumbed, so that it is not quite authentic by

Lunch for two in Abu Dhabi: Hammour and Chips

Yorkshire standards, though in its own right it is excellent. Lebanese potatoes being on the small side, the chips are a bit scrappy; but they are hot and without a trace of greasiness.

As usual, I arrive in the Middle East during Ramadan, the month of fasting from sunrise to sunset. So getting into the Golden Fish for lunch is like penetrating a Chicago speakeasy during Prohibition. I knock, whisper that Zaki has sent me, and then sit behind tightly drawn curtains, guiltily munching my chips as if they were ham sandwiches in Jerusalem. The manager tells me that business is fine. They opened in September 1971 and the word is spreading as far as Qatar and Kuwait. If you don't care for fish, there is sausage, egg and chips for 45p., or Lebanese *hommous*, Turkish coffee, and the usual international soft drinks. The frying range is Italian; dinky and efficient, but it wouldn't cope with the volume if this were, say, Blackpool.

The Golden Fish at next-door Dubai could not have been more aptly named, for Dubai is the heart of the Middle East gold traffic—the nicest little sheikhdom I know, with an airport out of fairyland and a seaport which is like Venice with dhows instead of gondolas. Dubai being a more compact and mature place than *nouveau riche* Abu Dhabi, its fish shop has already found a role in the community, as a resort for sheikhly teenagers and for some inexplicable white hippies in frayed jean shorts. The fish, the chips and the prices are the same as in Abu Dhabi, but the decor includes a ship's steering wheel and some once trendy posters of the Beatles, Bob Dylan and Carnaby Street. The frier wears a chef's hat and comes from Palestine.

The Persian Gulf, however, is only the latest annex of a Fish & Chips Imperialism which has been straining to spread its boundaries for at least half a century. In 1927, the omnipresent Chatchip reported a Fried Fish Boom in Germany. Almost overnight, no fewer than 188 shops had sprung up, with 24 in Berlin, 13 in Hamburg, 9 in Bremen, and others in Frankfurt, Dusseldorf and Mainz. Seeing that the Germans had no experience of the Trade and could not even enjoy the benefits of a German translation of his own manual, Chatchip thought they were doing remarkably well. To this day, I should add, there is a German Fish Friers' Association, particularly strong in the Anglophile, fish-catching north, and as my illustration shows, a Fish & Chip stall was a feature of the Cologne International Food Fair in 1969.

There have been sporadic outbreaks of Fish & Chips at holiday resorts in Belgium and Holland. But the fact is, between the French tradition of *pommes frites* and the Dutch and Scandinavian tradition of raw pickled herring, our fried fish and chips have not been able to root themselves firmly in Northern Europe. When one moves towards the Mediterranean, there are other handicaps: the potato does not compare with bread, rice and *pasta* as a regional staple, and the tiny local fish, although delicious in a crisply fried heap like autumn leaves, are simply not built to be filleted and dipped in batter.

However, the British invasion of the Spanish holiday coasts has had its impact. My special correspondent writes:

'Researches on the Costa del Sol, which is rather swish, proved chipless. That part of Spain is famous for its own fish snacks (*tapas*) and the little bars that specialize in them (*taskas*). And maybe your average exiled Nazi doesn't care for Fish & Chips. The chips in Spain fall mainly on the Costa Blanca, Franco's nearest approach to Blackpool: cheap package holidays with the charter flights bringing out continuous supplies of bottled beer as well as the dreadful working classes for their slap and tickle in the sun. There are a great many fish shops, British and Spanish owned, promising Fish & Chips just like Mum makes 'em (which, of course, she doesn't). The potatoes are Spanish and the chips indistinguishable from those in the average British shop. They don't use olive oil. The fish is local and mostly white. You can sit down and eat at a table, with a glass of beer, but if you want to take it away they wrap it in white plastic bags, not newspaper. The shops do a roaring trade with the British tourists (hardly any other nationality goes to places like Benidorm) but it appears that some of the Spaniards have taken to eating Fish & Chips, too.'

Malta and Cyprus (where there is an Andy Capp chain) cater authentically to the demands of the British serviceman, and so does Gibraltar. But work your way round to Greece, Turkey and the Levant and the local titbits tend to be either fried octopus or skewers of grilled meat and various forms of meat-ball or barbecue. The same is true through the Arab world and most of Africa, and in the meat-eating parts of India and Pakistan. For obvious reasons, fish is at a disadvantage in a hot climate, unless one is very near the water. The smell of fish frying is one of the characteristics of the river front in Vientiane, Laos; while the Bengalis (whose land is largely delta) are as devoted to fish as the Americans are to beef steak. But in neither area can a real Fish & Chip movement be descried. Just once, as I flashed through the streets of Bombay in a hurry to catch a plane, I glimpsed a sign that read 'Punjabi Fried Fish Centre—Buy Once, Return Often', but whether it sold chips as well as fish, I have never found out.

Tilapia: with Chips in Darkest Africa

There is Fish & Chips to be had in South Africa, although some whites look down on it as a favourite food of the 'coloured' or Eurafrican people of the Cape; and I have eaten Fish & Chips on the Thorn Tree

Myddleton Quality Fish Bar: note saveloys in case at left

The chip shop: a social centre for all ages

terrace of the New Stanley Hotel in Nairobi. The fish was *tilapia*, a Kenya lake fish, cut in the same chunky fingers as the Abu Dhabi *hammour*, and it was quite acceptable, although a trifle undercooked because of its thickness. A couple of hundred yards away, in Portal Street, the Red Rocks Bar & Restaurant was selling Fish & Chips, Sausage and Chips and Kebab and Chips for two shillings.

Rumours of Fish & Chips in Addis Ababa led me to expect that I should find the same sort of thing there. Potatoes should grow well on the Abyssinian highlands, and there are lakes to supply the fish. But no —the reports were just another example of our magic phrase being used to catch the eye. What in fact was happening was that a British frozen food company had organized a service of refrigerated vans across the five hundred miles of shattering country between the coast and Addis Ababa. Fish, chips, potted shrimp and kippers were among the deep frozen items being imported and eaten, mainly by the British community. So visions of the sons of Sheba lining up to buy a sizzling six-penn'orth, fried in a Nuttall twin-duct automatic and wrapped in the Amharic Times proved an illusion. In any case, I doubt whether the delicacy of fried fish will ever make much impact upon palates seared by *wat* and *injeera*—the howling local curry, eaten with cold crêpe-rubber bread.

Our trail gets warmer as we return to Union Jack country. There is a Chinese store in Suva, Fiji, where you can get Fish & Chips for lunch some days, provided the local police station hasn't bought it all up. In New Zealand, according to my informants, 'it's just like home', and so it is in British Columbia and Nova Scotia. But after personal investigation, it is to Australia that I must award my trophy, The Plastic Dogfish, for the world's *worst* Fish & Chips.

It was only to be expected, I suppose, in view of the strong Irish influence (which is always a handicap to food pleasure) and of the Australian insistence that it is unmanly to make a fuss about what you are eating. I will admit to having bought some quite tolerable Fish & Chips in Perth, Western Australia; but the frier had only recently immigrated from Britain and still had some standards of reference. But my experience in Sydney left me wondering whether there was some national consensus to mortify the stomach in order to lift the mind to higher things. It was my blackest moment in months of generally agreeable research.

Just one establishment in the neighbourhood of Fitzroy and Bourke Streets brought back memories of Camden Town. Most of the friers I visited seemed to be from the smaller autonomous republics of Jugoslavia which, through no fault of their own, are off the mainstream of the Fish & Chips tradition. Round King's Cross, I visited a number of cramped booths selling Hamburgers, Hot Dogs, Pasties, Chicken, and

Steak Sandwiches, as well as Fish & Chips—a menu far beyond their capacity to do well. Some offered chips and two pieces for 55 cents, others chips and one piece for 40. Although I made my visits at lunch or supper time, not a sizzle was to be heard in any of them—not once the sound of fresh portions being plunged into the pan. Everything I bought gave the impression of having been baked in the oven for half an hour. In some cases the chips were just passable, but the anonymous fish, described by one frier as 'Usually some kind of shark' and by another as 'Just fish', was dreadful beyond imagining. The flesh itself was dry and tasteless; the surrounding batter more like a plastic capsule, with a layer of uncooked batter between it and the fish. It left me groping for the words of some travel article I had read: 'Eating out in Sydney has reached new heights of sophistication with the arrival of exotic immigrant cuisines from the Mediterranean.'

The dream of launching Fish & Chips upon the United States is older than most people think. In 1935, *The Fish Trades Gazette* reported that Captain H. Auten (R.N.Ret'd), V.C., D.S.C., was trying to establish 'English Fish Bars' in New York, Chicago, San Francisco, Los Angeles, Boston and New Orleans. And the following year, the *Gazette* put on its worst pseudo-American twang to announce: 'It's a wow! You wanna step down to 130 East 45th Street and see a little bit of England in the form of a Fish & Chip shop? It's a cinch! New Yorkers who have dis-covered this dandy eat are sure spilling a bibful about it. It's the works!'

What it actually was was 'Cooper's Fish & Chips', a sitdown fish restaurant run by two entrepreneurs named Phil Cooper and George Gross. They sold fish, chips, bread and butter for the equivalent of one shilling. On their first day they served a thousand customers, turned away three hundred and banked £750. How long they lasted I do not know, but it would surprise me if, during the past fifty years, there had not always been some bright young man frying away in the English style somewhere in America. Certainly there was in 1960, when I encountered a fish shop near Monterey in California which, besides selling the traditional human meal, disposed of its fish scraps by selling them to its customers to feed to a sea-lion kept in a tank outside.

It must have been about five years after this that Haddon Salt—an enterprising young frier and range salesman from Skegness—opened *his* Fish & Chip shop in Sausalito. This is a small, swinging bay-side township across the Golden Gate Bridge from San Francisco, already much addicted to what Americans call 'seafood'. Salt gave his place a bowler hat, rolled umbrella 'I say, Old Boy' image, somewhat at variance with the true, working-class origins of our proletarian finger-food—but who was to know or care? Fish & Chips, folksified into 'Fish 'n Chips', was served in specially printed hygienic replicas of a front page of *The Times*, but the product was authentic and (in the early days) pretty good. Within four years, H. Salt Esquire boasted a chain of more than four hundred outlets, and the founder had sold out to the Kentucky Fried Chicken people, who had already bought out Colonel Sanders, and who in turn were taken over by a distillery group.

The later 1960s saw an astonishing expansion of the roadside Fast Food industry in America. People had more money to spend, and were driving about the country with it more than ever. More wives were working, or at least rebelling against the kitchen. The T.V. dinner had flopped, undermined by the tendency to promise more on the label than was actually in the box. And the old pattern of three meals a day at fixed times was breaking down. Into this confusion bustled highly systematized caterers like Burger Chef and MacDonald's with their hamburgers, the Colonel and his imitators with their fried chicken, Shakey's Pizza Parlors, Zum-Zum Sausage Bars, Doggie Diners, and a mob of Bar-B-Q Lodges, Pancake Pull-Inns, Hot Dog Havens, DoNut Drive-ups and Beef 'n Beans Chuck Waggons. Hamburgers rolled the fastest, followed by chicken, but Fish 'n Chips did well for a foreign import with nothing behind it by way of domestic precedent, save the dubious Southern tradition of the Negro catfish fry. I have seen placards in Alabama advertising 'All the Cats you can eat for $1.00'.

American give-away—British know-how

The biggest of the Fish & Chip chains to develop were H. Salt, Arthur Treacher's, Alfie's and Long John Silver's. But there was a host of smaller enterprises enabling me to indulge, once again, my passion for lists. To name only a few, there were:

Union Jack Fish & Chips
Olde English Fish 'n Chips
Lancashire Lad

London Fish & Chips
Moby Dick's Fish & Chips
London Bridge Fish n' Chips
Mr. Fish & Chips
The Hungry Cockney
Wee Willie Fish 'n Chips
London Bobby Fish 'n Chips
Hungry Penguin Fish & Chips
Yorkshire Fish & Chips Shoppe
Carnaby Fish & Chips
H.M.S. Cod
Captains' Choice Fish 'n Puppy*
Cedric's Fish & Chips
London Ben Fish & Chip Shoppe
Ye Old Country Squire
Ye Fish Chips 'n Ale

The general pattern of neo-Elizabethan quaintness will be all too clear. Arthur Treacher's employed as figure-head an elderly actor who, though virtually unknown in Britain, was widely assumed by Americans to have stepped out of the pages of P. G. Wodehouse. At the time of my researches, Alfie's was supplying a large portion of cod with chips for the equivalent of 35p., Long John Silver's for 42p. and Treacher's, who included a dollop of 'creamy cole slaw', for 48p.—though the size of the helpings was not necessarily the same in all cases.

Fanning the wildfire spread of Fish & Chips was the technique known as 'franchising'. In a nutshell, this means that instead of building the chain yourself, you sell the book of instructions to candidates who apply. They have to put up the money to build the shop, and they pay you 8 or 9 per cent of their gross takings. But you have to train them, supervise them, take care of the brand-name advertising, and pick up the pieces if your franchisee fails. In the American Trade, a franchisee might be expected to put down $5,000 as a basic fee, plus a down payment of $7,000 on about $27,000 worth of equipment. He still has his land and his building to pay for, though these, even with the all-important car park round them, are cheaper than in Britain. But the franchisee—once all this has been taken care of—should then find himself with a foolproof, guaranteed method of turning out a nationally famous product, and with no other outlet for miles around to compete with him.

From the inventor's point of view, the point of franchising is the rapid expansion of your name by using other peoples' capital. The disadvantages are several: unless your training methods are really foolproof and your system of checking up rigorous, any one of your friers

* *I hope and believe this means a 'hush-puppy' or fritter.*

could kill your name dead for ever as far as his district is concerned. And if he makes a success, you will be getting a much smaller return from your idea than if you had financed it yourself. The franchise system appealed to the traditional American philosophy of 'every man his own capitalist', but it disappointed the newer concept 'every corporation its own master'. Very soon, the chains adopted a policy of buying franchises back, and of putting in their own salaried managers.

Unfortunately this phase coincided with a general business recession in America. Some chains found their franchisees howling to be bought out when there was no money to buy them with; others were begging franchisees to buy out the company, sometimes for as little as a dollar. Some friers blamed the collapse on an ecological scare about fish being contaminated with mercury (a Mercury Fish Bar in Detroit had to be quickly renamed), but the fact was that like other American crazes before, Fish & Chips had been blown up too big, too fast. Of the major chains, Arthur Treacher's rode the storm best; partly because its expansion had been selective and controlled, but also because its technical adviser was Denis Malin of the reputedly 'oldest Fish & Chip shop in Britain'. Whether it is the oldest or not, Malin, still in his forties, is an impressive example of a new generation reaching the top in the old Trade, a generation prepared to take on the United States or anywhere else. He talks of the possibilities in Germany and Japan next.

The trouble with America, Denis Malin thinks, is that since most people live so far from the sea, they aren't naturally 'fish orientated'. They don't care for a real fish flavour, and they are easily distracted by batter, to which they attach more importance than the fish. It is hard to tell where Fish & Chips will succeed in the United States. Down the East Coast and among the 'ethnic groups'—that is, the continental European immigrants—of the industrial states like Ohio, excellent business has been done. 'We've had $12,000 a week from a small shop in Cleveland, though $8,000 is more typical.' Idaho and Montana have been unexpected successes. But in Texas it didn't go too well. Malin thinks one reason for the failure of the other chains was that they paid off their British advisers too soon and allowed too many individual variations in the product. Friers weren't supervised closely enough, and some of them even cut their own fish and potatoes, which calls for 'tremendous expertise'.

Denis Malin's method (which is patented) leaves nothing whatever to chance: it is drummed into the trainees who attend the one-week course at headquarters in Columbus. 'Basically,' he says, 'it is a system that fifteen-year-olds or *monkeys* could operate. We take the frozen fish out of the ice-box and *temper* it a bit, still keeping it solid—to thaw fish out is like cutting its jugular vein. Then there's the question of batter. We use corn-flour—maize flour—and each batch has a viscosity of its own which has to be carefully checked. We weigh it, and the water, and even control the temperature because if it heats, it thins. The correct size and weight of the fish portion called for a lot of trial and error at first, but not any more. You drop it in. It sinks to the bottom. And when it rises to the top with every part floating, you know it is cooked to perfection. Of course that's coupled with the correct temperature of the peanut oil, the batter, the fish—all put together, step by step and foolproof. If you thawed the fish out it would float much sooner, so having it almost solid acts as an indicator. If I get someone who's used to food, their intelligence is insulted by the simplicity. If I have trouble, it's usually with someone who thinks.'

Malin has even evolved a new chip for the Americans: 'The half-inch square chip had been used for years and years. We wanted something different. So we got what they call a steak fry, which is three-quarters' of an inch wide, three-eighths thick, like an oblong. This wasn't very appealing to Americans who like their chips very crisp; but after a while they realized they hadn't been tasting the potatoes, just the crispness. Then our chip caught on, but it did tend to sag a bit. Now I've developed one in the style of a crinkle-cut, but with the grooves going lengthways down the chip instead of across it. It took me nine months to get and it's functional as well as attractive. The peaks of the grooves get toasted and that gives it strength as well as colour. Even if it gets a little cool, it's still crisp when you bite it. We refer to it as "the French Fry with the Baked Potato Taste".'

North Atlantic White Fish: just plain cod

Nor does Malin take any chances with his raw materials. The five million pounds of fish Treacher's use every year, they get from Iceland; the Canadians cannot yet keep up a consistent quality. They use cod exclusively, but often have to call it 'North Atlantic White Fish', because cod to Middle Westerners only means cod-liver oil. As for the chips: 'We use frozen chips—it's absolutely necessary where they haven't the experience to know when to blanch or soak them. Every batch of potatoes that comes in from the fields has a different sugar content and will cook differently if you don't do something about it. So the chips are semi-boiled twice in water, until the sugar is reduced below the standard level we want. Then they add sugar to bring it up to the level, and all those chips will cook identically, the same colour. So in the shop they're frozen solid; we don't temper them, we just put them in the pan, press the timer, and they come out when they're perfect.

'We teach our trainees never to put hot fish or chips on top of cold fish or chips. We never enclose them in a hot box, but if they've been sitting out under the heater, we throw them away after ten minutes for fish, five minutes for chips. I don't like these times, but the situation is very different from Britain.'

Treacher's use American ranges which are more successful for the 'continuous flow' method the chain uses. 'We have to maintain a much better temperature control than the traditional English frier, who loads the pan, sees the temperature drop, and takes it on the uplift. We don't do that, because we're frying as the demand comes in. It takes only five minutes to cook the fish and three minutes for the chips, so the instant the car drives into the parking lot, the frier drops in four portions. You've got to keep an eye on that parking lot.'

As cashiers, Treacher's pick the all-American girls who laugh at every joke the instructor makes. They're the ones who chirrup 'Y'all hurry back, y'hear?' as you end your one and only visit in a lifetime to Hygiene, Colorado. They've also got to be very, very careful girls, because their cash registers are set to make an hourly analysis of sales, and one copy of the tape goes to Columbus, so that headquarters know what's going on and what their percentage is. 'When I go trouble-shooting,' says Denis Malin, 'I walk into the shop knowing what's wrong in advance. It's very impressive.'

11. A Company of Friers

Like a Public House, a Fish & Chip shop is only as good as the man (and woman) who runs it. Indeed, the dependence is even closer, for the frier at his best is a craftsman as well as a host: he prepares his wares as well as serving them; and the traditional frier who began his day (as some still do) selecting fresh cod at Billingsgate and ended it frying till midnight, needed good humour, stamina and skill in equal proportions. Like a good Pub landlord, he is an individualist who comes from the masses, serves them and identifies with them, and yet is set apart from them by his work. Depending, like the landlord, upon the regular patronage of neighbours, he may eventually become something of an 'uncle figure', a self-caricature. He derives deep satisfaction from the very act of feeding people, almost as if it were a sacerdotal function. Here, from my notebooks and tape-recordings is a selection of such men:

George Mayston, Old Ford
Strictly speaking, George isn't a frier at all. But at the age of ninety-eight, having walked a-mile-and-a-half to Malin's for his Fish & Chips since he was ten years old, he is my oldest witness and I crave the indulgence of the court. He has the centuries-old dignity of King Rameses in the Cairo Museum:

'Along here there used to be a stable for the horse buses; and if you found twenty used tickets and took them along, the hostler would give you a free haircut with the horse shears. If you gave the driver of those buses a penny stinker cigar, he'd let you ride up beside him. Those days, there was boot-black boys and horse-dung boys, crossing sweepers and German bands and a man who played the harp on the corner outside Malin's. We boys used to suck lemons at the German band to make their mouths water. And there used to be an Italian organ grinder with a little organ that stood on one leg, and a monkey on the top—a nice little thing. But the monkey was as artful as the Italian; he pulled my hair and wouldn't let go till I gave him a penny. In those days a builder's labourer got fourpence ha'penny an hour, and thirty shillings a week went a long way. You could get a dozen Dutch oysters for one-and-six-pence.

'The fish at Malin's was just wrapped in newspaper. They had very strong vinegar then, and we used to take a big swig of it. Malin's only had steamer fish, from the trawlers that steamed up to Billingsgate; and they only took the first boxes off the top. You never got a bad fish here.'

Faulkner's 'Kensington': dignity with a condenser-box in 1910

Albert Malin, Old Ford

At seventy-eight, Albert Malin looks like a respectable Old Steptoe, and on Fridays he still puts on his white coat and does his stint in the family shop. He was born in a Fish & Chip shop, and so was his son:

'On a Saturday, my Mum and Dad used to fry up some chips and go to bed for a rest and leave me and my brother in charge: eleven and twelve years of age. If we ran out of fish we used to fry up a new lot. Can you imagine what the authorities would say today? I actually won a three-year scholarship, but my father didn't believe in it. I had to leave school at fifteen. But they did send me to a Higher School at Queens Road—a very good school with mixed classes. We had a teacher there called Warminster, a proper little dandy. If there was any difficulty, you went up to him at his desk for a bit of private tuition. But I only done it once. I went up there, and as I got there he called out: "That's near enough—don't come any closer!"—because of the smell. I was put up at a desk in a corner where the window was; you did smell, you see, no pan-covers in those days and the oil wasn't purified. Some of those Jewish people used to stink terrible. There was a lot of Jewish friers then—flooded the trade. We didn't get many Italians in London, but now it's all Cypriots.

'In the old days, we never had this dirty fish—skate and dogfish—never used 'em. All we ever had was Scarborough cod, North Sea plaice direct from Lowestoft, and haddock. We had beautiful cod steaks—no fillets, people wouldn't eat fish without the bone, and the old-timers still won't—our steaks were ha'penny and three-farthings each. My father was very particular about his plaice. He used to have two boxes from a man named Wisker of Lowestoft, and they had to be all male fish. They had to be 'pound and a quarter to 'pound and a half, and there was a limit on the price: one-and-six to two-and-three a stone. If they was half a crown, he sent them back as too dear. They used to cut all beautiful middles—'penny, three-ha'pence and tuppence—a tuppenny was a select customer in those days. Fish? You don't even get it today!

'When I was about ten—in them days what you used for rock fish was monkfish, beautiful fish. If they used any rock at all, it was monk. The first lot of catfish we ever got was fourpence a stone—lovely stuff, straight off the Dogger Bank. We were probably one of the first to use it as rock salmon. My father used Egyptian cottonseed oil; we all used it. You did get a bit of a smell, but it held its body so well . . .

'Chips? My father used to get little King Edwards in pea bags, hundredweight-and-a-quarter for ninepence a bag when new. We had a great big tub in the yard and used to sit round cutting them up by hand. My father gave us threepence a bag towards our holiday money. I don't know anybody that peeled potatoes in those days. We used to put them in the tub with a couple of half-bricks and churn them with an old mop. Peeling machines weren't in general use till after the First War. You just had an open range with two pans like old coppers. In them days you had no lids over the pans, no ventilators; they just opened the windows . . .

'With the terrible price fish is now, I'm glad I'm out of it. In the old days, if they didn't like the price, they didn't buy fish; the friers would just go into the Cock and booze, and come home all boozed with no fish. When they tried to put the oil up to fifteen shillings a hundredweight, all the friers met down in the market and broke 'em; they got 'em back to nine. They just wouldn't buy none. That was just after 1900—though, mind you, there wasn't the competition in those days . . .

'I know my father and my grandfather would decide to go to Clacton on a Sunday and perhaps stop the Monday, too. They'd put a golden sovereign on the mantelpiece under one of the vases. Then they knew they could spend all they'd got in their pockets, because they'd put away their stock money for the morning's fish. So long as they had enough money under the vase to go to market next morning, that was all they worried about.

'What are the secrets of good frying? Really it's hard to say. You can only judge the temperature of your pan, see your batter's not puddingy and put it in the right way.

'People still love their Fish & Chips. Go into a caff for a meal—open the door and it'll blow away! Order a piece of meat, and they just show it to you . . .'

Joe Lees, Mossley.

At eighty, Joe Lees still remembers his grandfather John Lees who founded 'The Oldest Chip Potato Establishment in the World', circa 1863. Joe shows me a photograph of himself on his grandfather's knee:

'He were drunk at time—and me with me clogs and jam butty . . . Me grandfather was one of the lads; he liked his beer; he had t'much. Once he said to his wife: "Give me a hundred quid and I'll go out of your life for ever." She thought it would be the best spent hundred quid she'd ever laid out, so she gave him all she had. In three weeks he were back. He'd been to London and gone through the bottom wi' booze. "Besides," he said, "you only give me ninety quid—not a hundred." Oh, he were a villain!

'The first thing I can remember about me grandfather's old shop was when they pulled it down and I took some firewood home for me mother. It were just a little wood hut selling chip potatoes. And me grandmother made pea soup. You could have a bowl of soup and a muffin. I heard a lad go in one night and he said: "Mrs. Lees, d'you put pig feet into this soup?" She says, "Yes, lad." He said, "It's kicked all t'peas out, then."

'Now, the first chip shop as we knew about was this man in Oldham; and that's how me grandfather got this idea; and when he opened this hut, "In the French and American Style" it said over the door. This were a gimmick, you see. This man who had this place in Oldham, he left it and went to keepin' a public house called The White Bear; and it's been demolished years ago.

Resemblance to Mr. Enoch Powell, an accident

The BETTER CLASS DRIPPING

(It sparkles with Purity).

Each Box of our

DRIPPING

is

GUARANTEED

PURE

and if you are not delighted with it when you have given it a Trial we will refund your MONEY cheerfully and without Question.

Established 1840.

'In those days there was no chip ranges like there is today. We used to have the old "Shet pot"—they're a boiler, really, what they used to boil the clothes. And they used dripping in those days; but after we got a proper chip range we cooked in cottonseed oil. There was a certain time of the year when it had a peculiar smell, as if you were burning wood.

'D'you know how much fish was when I started? Seven for sixpence: cod or hake. And d'you know what I bought hake at? Fourteen pound for fourpence ha'penny sometimes. And people wouldn't eat it. It was all cod round about here those days.

'After me grandfather there were four sons: Tom, Squire, Channing, Father—and two daughters in the business. We'd six shops. My father bought a shop in Manchester for eighty pound. D'y'know what we took? Twenty pound a week—that were takings, not profit—we were working for nothing, really. And we did three sessions: eleven-thirty till one, dinnertime; four till six, teatime; and half-past eight till eleven, suppertime. There were five shops on Stratford Road, two on this side, two on that, and we was in the middle. But we sold more than the other four put together when we got movin' . . .

'Stratford Road—police went about in twos, and I got knocked down a few times. There was this chap in t'shop using some awful language, so me Dad got 'old of 'im, he never 'it 'im, but the longer he stuck the further 'is tongue came out. 'e were goin' black in t'face, when me Dad gets 'im up against stone jamb outside of shop and BOP! on 'is 'ead. Then one of t'gang 'appened to leg me father, and I could see this fist coming and went on me back in tramlines. When police came round, I said, "Where t'hell's tha been?" "Well," he said, "Tha shouldn't have come outside. If you've any bother, hit him with something hard while he's in t'shop, and then send for me. If you do it outside, you're as bad as him."

'This shop across the road—it were only a young fellow that managed it—and 'e says to me: "Now gang'll come to *my* shop!" I says, "Very likely; but I'll tell you what police told me: 'it 'em with something 'ard while they're inside."

'Saturday night, I could 'ear Bobbies' whistles going. When I saw 'im next, I asked 'ow did it go? "Ooh," he said, "I'm like to be 'ad up for murder." I says, "Why?" He says, "That gang come into my shop and were playing 'ell with piano; so I just went in and said to cut that out. 'Who art tha talkin' to?' So I just picked a fourpenny bit (that's what they called them tall wooden stools) and clocked him one on t'napper."

'I said, "What were Bobbies doing?" "Takin' 'im to hospital to have his head stitched." "And how are you goin' on?" "Oh," he says, "when police came round takin' particulars they said: 'Was it in self-defence?' 'Oh, yes,' I says, 'self-defence!' But really, it weren't that; I durstn't give 'im chance to 'it me—so I 'it 'im first . . ."

'Chap I knew very well came to me one day, he said: "D'y'know I'm going in t'fish trade?" I said, "Where?" He says, "Oldham." "Oh, well," I says, "anything you want to know, like . . ."'

'He went on the Monday. He came into my shop the Wednesday night. He says, "Tha knows that shop ah bawt?" (We all talked in t'dialect, just like that.) "Well, wife doin' t'cookin'—shoved that job on to 'er for a start—well, when she puts fish into t'pan, they won't come to top. They all stick at bottom in one big loomp." I says, "Listen, when your missus has cooked as many as me, you'll just drop it in Kch! and it'll come up. Your fat's not hot enough. And how are you goin' on otherwise?" He says, "Not so good." First week, how much d'you think they took? Thirty bob! And he tell me: "Tha knows there's a chap comes in t'other day and says, "ow long's tha been 'ere?' 'Ooh, Ah've only been in about a week.' 'Well,' he says, 'Tha knows, them as flits out—I've got t'job of flittin' 'em. Either takin' away furniture to ware'ouse, or takin' people to work'ouse.'" That chap, 'e were back in Mossley in 'is old house before they'd put anyone else into it.'

'In the First World War, in France, they were just like ice-cream barrers selling chip potatoes. They had just one pan, and they used to stand on what they called the Grand Place (that's the market ground), specially at Lille. There used to be five or six of them. "Pom-di-terr frips," or something like that. At Mons there were tables and cubicles; a big place, with salt and vinegar, but no fish . . .'

The vanishing hake: annihilated by Spaniards

Maurice Williams, Truro.
A big, paunchy man with a boxer's head of curly black hair, Maurice Williams decided in his mid-forties that he had 'made his pile' and was selling out. He is a Nottingham man, but courted his wife in Truro during his Navy days, and promised her a bungalow on the very hillside where they live today. They are a house-and garden-proud couple, and drive a smart plum-coloured Rover:

'My father lived in a two-up, two-down, toilet-at-the-bottom-of-the-yard cottage in Nottingham. He did a twelve-hour day, six days a week at the cycle works for two-pounds-ten to three pounds a week. I followed after him and started at twenty-four shillings a week.

'At school, at exams, it just didn't come. All my reports show I was a trier, but it just didn't come then. I got out of the cycle works and went to work for Imperial Tobacco, at Players, and although that was better I couldn't see any opening. There was too many bloody people in the way. I didn't want to be a millionaire, but I didn't want to be counting my money for fags, or spending money on beer that I couldn't afford. After the Navy, I went back to tobacco at four-pound-ten a week. I couldn't bloody breathe...

'As a lad, I used to go and buy two penn'orths of chips for me and my brother and watch Mr. and Mrs. Smith doing chips. It was mostly chips —they had fish, but they only cooked it to order. Mrs. Smith, who did most of the frying, even had a real Fish & Chips voice—all dried up. Mr. Smith was a coalminer; he used to prepare the stuff at night and took great pride in peeling and eyeing his potatoes to perfection. He was doing a job that was fascinating; his batter was crisp and light, and I'ld give up my turn just to watch him cooking. He singled me out, and I knew I could do it some day, because Mr. Smith had shown me how.

'One day, my mother-in-law wrote and said "Mr. N—— is selling his shop". This was January 1947. So I raised the fare down to Truro and went round to ask the price. He said, £2,500, all fitted, freehold, with a four-roomed flat above. (Mr. N——'s Fish & Chips were all right, but they weren't like Mr. Smith's.) All I had was £40. I went into L——'s Bank, though I couldn't even fill in a cheque in those days, and it was the first time I'd been in a bank at all. "Can't help you, my handsome," the man said. I almost cried. Then I saw B——'s Bank opposite, and I thought "Remember Mr. Smith—don't give up!" The manager there said: "Sit down, my handsome." And there I was, an upcountry bloody bloke, asking for money. "That's all right," said the manager, "Freehold, is it? How much have you got?" "Forty quid," I says. "Can you make it two hundred?" I says, "Yes." "Then ask Mr. N—— for his audited accounts for the past three years, and find yourself a guarantor and some life assurance."

'So my mother-in-law tells me to go and see an uncle who was a building contractor and a customer of the bank, and he walks in to see the manager. 'You will do, Mr. K——," says the manager, "you will do." So I gives Mr. N—— his ten per cent down, and gets a piece of paper off him which I gives to the bank. Next day, Mr. N—— says to me, "Here's your cheque back; and I'm sorry, but someone offered me £500 more." I told the bank manager, "It's all off"; but he says: "You tell Mr. N—— he's sold it to you, and I've got this bit of paper to prove

Fish and Chips invade Germany: President Braun of the German Friers'
Association greets President Arnold Scholes, long-running President of the
British Friers. 1969

Top   Abu Dhabi's Golden Fish: furtive chips during Ramadan
Bottom   Dubai: Sheikhs' delight on a Friday night

it." And so it was—though I had to argue with the solicitor later to get him to cut his charges.

'Our first two years were very hard. Supplies were still rationed and we could only open Wednesdays and Fridays with five stone of hake each day. It was twelve-and-six a stone and potatoes twelve-and-six a hundredweight, all government-controlled. When there wasn't any hake they'ld send what they called Scotch hake. It ate all right, but it never came with a head on it, and once when it did it had strange whiskers . . . Our first week, we sold £21. Our best day's take was £8.

'Sometimes we had to shut up shop for lack of fat, and I had to go to Bristol to argue with the Fats and Oils Office. The only way you could get more was through one of these "Strachey Licences" which gave you four hundredweight every eight weeks where there was "unsatisfied consumer need". I got one by agreeing to take a mobile round the villages—the Food Office told me which ones: Playing Place, Quenchwell, Perranwell, Feock, Keye—outlandish bloody places, but these were the terms of my licence.

'I got a Ford V8 and drove it up to Cardiff and got Preston and Thomas to put a coal range in it. And on days when the shop was shut, we did our round. I prepared a timetable and we tried to keep to it, though being about the only thing off the ration in those days, we kept getting waylaid along the road, especially by holiday-makers.

'That mobile helped us along, but it was bloody dangerous. We were stoking fires in a moving vehicle full of hot fat. And we had to be careful where we stopped. There were two outlets for smoke and two for steam, and they had to be aimed the right way. Sometimes, going along, the trees would knock the cowls over and fill the whole van with smoke. We went to Malpas, a mile down the river from Truro, and the harbour-master came after us saying our smoke was a danger to navigation.

'The end came just after I painted the vehicle up. We were stopped at the top of a hill near Perranwell. Now, there was a woman with several kids that used to meet us at the *bottom* of the hill, and if we weren't up to frying heat, the kids would climb all over the van while we burned up a bit. So I said this time we'ld stop at the *top* and fry up a batch to serve right away at the bottom, so the kids wouldn't scratch the new paintwork.

'Well, we were pointing a bit downhill, and when I put in a basket of chips, the oil bubbled up and over, down the front of the range and into the ash tray. It shot up all ruddy orange and black. We carried a fire extinguisher, but it was of no avail. I saved all I could, but by the time the fire brigade arrived, it was all down to the chassis. The vehicle was insured, but not the fittings. We lost a packet and it shook us up a bit.

'If you think you know it all in the Trade, you're in trouble. Frozen portions—they're too standardized. When I cut 'em, each one is an individual; on the rack, they look like real little fish. But when you see those frozen portions on the rack, it looks like a builder's yard after a demolition. We can't rely on glossy packaging. We've got to put the appeal into each portion. There's been a lot of problems with frozen portions—the crystals blowing the batter off. They have to use a special batter, more like a tasteless concrete mixture. And the oil has to have a low temperature, or the batter cooks before the fish. So you virtually boil the fish in oil, which gives you a tough batter.

'Then you can get "stinkers". A "stinker" is a fish that's eaten something that disagrees with it. It's not too bad to eat, but it smells awful, like cat's piddle. In one frozen portion you can get bits of all sorts of different fish, and one might be a stinker. Put a frozen bit in the pan and it sinks to the bottom like a log. Mine bounce straight up to the surface again.

'There's much less anti-chips snobbery than there used to be. I've had the Chief of Police and the Canons from the Cathedral in my place. I'm obsessed with cleanliness, and in my shops I have the walls and ceilings and fluorescent tubes washed once a week. I open at eleven-thirty and get away about two a.m. It's a race against the clock all the time...'

Leonidas Onoufriou, Camden Town.

LEO'S FISH BAR stands where the Liffey meets the Aegean, within sight of British Rail's huge, grey Camden Road viaduct. The area is not just cosmopolitan, it is interracial. The shop stands amidst battered terraces that can never, at their best, have been really fashionable; but to Leo, it is on the fringes of the West End, and he fancies he detects an occasional tourist among his customers. What he would really like is to see big blocks of council flats, or maybe a large office block, to repopulate the area and send three or four hundred hungry workers into the street every lunch hour.

Leo is a Greek Cypriot. As a child of seven he had to help in his uncle's restaurant to earn his lunch, so catering is 'in the blood'. Leo actually served five years' apprenticeship as a tailor, and came to London after the Second World War. About nine years ago, he noticed this shop in Camden Town; it had a coal-fired range still, and no extractor fan. Leo, who had the cash saved up, saw the business could be built up and offered to buy. 'No,' said the owner, 'I mean to die here like my father and grandfather before me.' But finally he broke down, admitting he had almost nothing to sell—a mere £40 a week turnover.

Leo bought it cheap, spent £10,000 gutting and re-equipping the shop. He has a Preston and Thomas range from Cardiff, which he worships, and which takes the fumes away into the basement and then blows them up over the rooftops, boosted by a fan. There is hardly a whiff of Fish or Chips in the shop.

Leo did have one other shop, but his arch-enemy, the Council, allowed a competitor to start up right next door. They kept doing that, he claims, so that there were two laundrettes, two tobacconists, two butchers, all side by side killing each other in the name of competition. In this case it was Leo who went to the wall and lost £7,000. But he had his revenge later, when another Greek fish bar opened up down the road from his existing premises. This time, Leo was the survivor.

Leo says it is very hard work. He begins at 9.30 a.m. and goes on without a break until midnight or 1.30 a.m. He has a woman and a young man from Ulster to help him, but they go off in the afternoon while Leo lingers on, reluctant to miss one more order. He clearly loves his role as a neighbourhood figure; he loves to see children grow up, get married and still keep coming to his shop. He himself has two daughters married—one to a 'half-Irish, half-Jewish fellow, very intelligent', the other to a 'pure English boy, but they've emigrated themselves to Australia'. All he asks, he says, is to clear £30 or £40 a week. This would give him a profit of £2,000 a year, which is not a big salary for such long hours—especially when you remember that it is also the interest on his capital.

What you really must have, says Leo, is a sense of timing. You don't want to have empty cases when a customer walks in; but you don't want to have full ones turning hard and dry. You've got to have extra sensitivity for things like what day of the week it is, the weather, the T.V. programmes, the counter-attractions. One recent Saturday he was suddenly £24 down: 'They'd all just been paid, the weather turned fine, so they all took off for the country.'

Leo 'phones his fish merchant every night for the next day's supplies: he won't use frozen fish on any account. He is very proud of his small haddock 'on the bone', which he has to trim and finish cleaning himself. Skate, too, needs a lot of preparation and by the time you've cut and skinned it, you can make a loss at present prices. Leo will cook *only* in groundnut oil and has a horror of dripping. Dripping, he says (acting out the consequences), sticks your lips together, is bad for the heart and it smells.

12. Whither the National Dish?

here could hardly be anything more twenty-first century than a Carry-Out Convenience Fast Food, which is exactly what Fish & Chips have been for the past hundred years. The Trade ought to have a head start in what has been declared the Fast Food Revolution. And yet it is full of doubts and fears; and with good reason.

The basic dish is beyond question. One might change a few frills, like offering wedges of lemon instead of the barbarous malt vinegar; and one may have to accept saithe and sea bream instead of cod and haddock. But otherwise, fish fried in batter is going to remain fish fried in batter. Yet as a foodstuff, fish (the senior partner in our duet) remains vulnerable. The housewife still regards it as optional, something to have 'for a change', and at most once a week. Incorrectly, she thinks it is more difficult to prepare than meat, and she is worried about freshness and smell.

The time is certainly gone when fish could be identified with the poor. On the contrary, one of its big problems in Britain is the risk of being priced into the luxury class; in which case the back-street, working-class Fish & Chip shop would vanish, or turn to a substitute, and only a specialist Seafood Restaurant would survive. The problem is worldwide, but it is particularly acute for Britain, whose own catching and frying industries have helped to set us high standards as the leading fish-eaters in the North Atlantic community. The significance of the quarrel over the Icelandic fishing limits is twofold: first, as a reminder that we are long past being able to supply our own needs from our own waters, and second, as a token that fish are now a world commodity over which the price offered by the United States is the dominant influence. So it is not surprising that, far above the grumbles concerning Chinamen and mobile chip vans, the central issue for the National Federation of Friers is the price and supply of fish.

However, fish is not the only food caught in the price tornado. One reason why the friers welcome the Common Market is that while it should not have much immediate impact upon the price of fish or potatoes, it is bound to increase the prices of competing foodstuffs. The result would be to make Fish & Chips look relatively cheaper. Moreover if, as seems to be the case, fish is becoming more and more a processed food, with fewer and fewer fishmongers selling wet fish direct to the housewife, the frier should be able to get the pick of what there is on the dockside. Already, of all the cod landed in Britain, 40 per cent goes into prepared fish-cakes, fish fingers and crumbed fillets, and 40 per cent to the friers. Only 20 per cent is sold wet on the slab.

White Fish Authority dream: Chips are thicker than Rice

Anyone who can remember their local High Street over the past twenty years can testify not only to the disappearance of the fishmonger, but to the striking growth of eating-out facilities during that time. It is not just the Indian, Chinese and Italian restaurants, but the Steak Bars, Pizza counters and takeaway shops of all kinds that have moved in, often into locations where Fish & Chips dared not tread. The new-comers do not seem to have captured much of the business previously done by the Trade; they have taken advantage of generally expanding conditions not unlike those found in the United States, and they have created new demands by offering new dishes. Yet some of their business has been business that Fish & Chips might have had (had it been there), and the Trade is now asking itself how it should react.

There are two obvious possibilities. One is that the existing type of family shop should diversify and attempt to pull in the curry and chicken custom. Years ago, in the East End of London, meat pie shops were as common as Fish & Chips; contemporaries of mine like Louis Heren can recall the steamed pies with white, salty gravy, and there are still a few shops that sell them to this day. Pies and peas have always been the first alternatives in a Fish & Chip shop. Few people make their own pies now. The mass-produced articles—though they will not bear serious examination as purveyors either of pleasure or of nourishment—are easy to store and heat, steady in price and wide in profit-margin. An alternative is the pasty, though I would never touch one east of the Tamar myself. There are appalling curries (or rather, spiced sauces to be poured over anything from chips to pieces of warmed-up meat), sickly saveloys (a kind of foam-filled sausage originally made from pig's brains), and various unidentifiable rissoles and fritters. There are parodies of Chinese dishes, which are said to give a profit seven times as high as an honest portion of fish. And there is chicken, though the flood of electrically driven 'rotisseries' has dropped below its high-water mark.

The effects of the trend to diversify, and so escape complete dependence on fish prices, can be seen in a W.F.A. survey showing that more than 50 per cent of friers possessed orthodox ovens, 16 per cent microwave ovens, and 25 per cent rotary spits. Only 1 per cent had the kind of griddle-plate commonly used for hamburgers. (However, the sample upon which this was based was, perhaps, too small to be quite reliable.)

The debate on whether it is really wise to diversify will go on until the last frier but one lays down his chip basket. The wisdom of the elders is: 'Pies—maybe. But once you go further than that, your Fish & Chips will suffer and the whole purpose of your existence is gone.' Even one of the new chain managers remarked: 'You can always tell when a Fish & Chip shop is slipping: it starts to diversify its menu in all directions in the hope of improving sales. But it doesn't. It just splits up the old takings among a lot of distracting lines.' But from a young planner in the Trade I heard another view: 'Why stay old-fashioned when you can buy an adequate array of rotisseries, pie heaters, microwave ovens, grills and a small Valentine frier—all of it taking up half the space of a conventional three-pan range, and for half the price?' Certainly the cost of sophisticated modern ranges is enough to frighten off the mere dabbler nowadays. It is all a matter, I should say, of where you are setting up business and what you intend to be. Maybe, with a Valentine the size of a small washing machine, you will never fry up to Harry Ramsden's standards. But over depressingly large areas of Britain south of Wolverhampton, few people will know or care. The American Fish Sandwich, essentially a large fish finger in a bun with a slice of cheese to give it some flavour, should be just the thing for the Motorway Age.

The Hamburger—begging Wimpy's pardon—has yet to hit Britain fair and square. In its true American form of unadulterated, government-graded, minced beef steak, I doubt if it ever will (outside expensive exceptions like Chelsea's 'Great American Disaster'). After generations of fobbing the public off with amalgams of snout, ears, tails, cheeks and dewlaps, not to mention liberal fillings of rusk, crumb and soya, British food manufacturers are hardly likely to revise their standards so drastically. The public, we are told, wouldn't like it and couldn't afford it. Nevertheless there is a hole in the menu, somewhere above the Wimpy and below the Berni rump steak, and both Denis Malin and the Seafarer chain are working to fill it.

Which brings us to the competition from Southern, Maryland, Kentucky or Dixie fried chicken. This requires almost as much care and equipment as fish-frying. It is no easy sideline for the small family shop. The chicken is prepared in a pressure cooker which resembles a small nuclear reactor, so that the skin caramelizes and the thin batter, flavoured with ''erbs and spices' impregnates the otherwise bland and tasteless flesh. You also need a special heat-humidified cabinet to store the pieces in, but they will keep for up to half an hour, compared with the decent maximum of ten minutes for fish.

A patented process like this calls for chain or franchise operation. Whether franchising in the American style will catch on in Britain, I doubt. It is relatively more expensive for the small man to franchise a worthwhile, large-volume shop in Britain; and the United States example has not encouraged British companies to travel the same road with such reckless abandon. It is significant that Seafarer's biggest expansion, in the North of England, has been through a group of sixty outlets, all in partnership with the same brewery. Few individuals could raise the £20,000 a shop may call for.

The growth of the chain shops (some of them franchised) is already clear to see. In the past couple of years, John Lyons' Wimpy Bars and Bake 'n Takes, and Associated Fisheries' Seafarers, have been joined by Kentucky Frieds, Pizzalands, Golden Kitchens, Cook Inns, Beef Trees and Wishing Bones galore—some eat-ins, some carry-outs, some both, but all emphasizing convenience and trouble-saving, and all ultimately dependent on that narrow book of instructions that even monkeys or part-time teenagers can follow. It is a far cry from the traditional frier's Rule of Thumb.

If the Fish & Chip shop is to join the gathering competition in the High Street—planning restrictions permitting—it is not going to be a cosy family shop any more, with takeaway facilities only, arbitrary opening times and standards of appearance all its own. People out shopping are going to want to sit down to eat, and that means hiring staff and opening up a whole new vista of woe to the proprietor. It is almost certainly going to mean that the family no longer lives over the shop and knows all its customers by name; and that the shop front and the interior decor will have to keep up with that of Jones & Son next door. And whether they like it or not, more and more family shops are having to move *somewhere*, as slum clearance and city development catches up with them and tears them down.

What the reborn family shop will find itself competing with is something along the lines of Seafarer, whose headquarters shop is in Notting Hill, in West London. On 28th January 1972, I found Cod and Chips at 27p. (served at the table), Haddock and Chips 28p., Plaice and Chips 32p., two pieces of Southern Fried Chicken and Chips 30p., Portion of Chips 8p., and a glass of Chablis 20p.

The colour scheme was predictably blue-and-white with wood for

From Associated Fisheries brochure

What does the Seafarer Franchise offer?

The Seafarer franchise is a total package professionally designed to help hard working, but inexperienced people realize the profit potential in the Fast Food market. You will get:

SEAFARER'S TEN POINT PLAN

* Area exclusivity
* Professional site selection advice
* Store design and shop fitting manual
* A complete equipment package
* 2 Week Training School Course
* Professional advertising support
* Better buying terms
* Mutual trading support
* Comprehensive Operations Manual
* Financing assistance

Above all you know that the successful experience of Seafarer over the past 6 years, and the specialist management team who have built it, are there to help solve your problems!

warmth, *à la Rogers*, and there were eel-and-pie-shop stalls to sit in. The General Manager of the chain, A. G. Williams, admits that the indecision about whether it is a humble takeaway or a posh restaurant induces a certain 'environmental schizophrenia'.

Williams argues that with service costs so substantial in this kind of establishment, the rising price of fish can to some extent be absorbed by seeing that it is a thoroughly efficient operation with really big volume. Notting Hill is not, in fact, Seafarer's star turn. With average weekly volume in the Trade around £250, Harry Ramsden's does an incredible £8,000 and the Seafarer at Basildon, £2,000, which is the kind of thing they're aiming at. Seen from Seafarers, the scruffier businesses are going down to the Cypriots, while the better ones are moving up towards the chains.

So, how to run this 'thoroughly efficient' Fish & Chip shop? For a start, Seafarer is part of a vertically integrated operation, with the same company, Associated Fisheries, handling the fish from the day it is caught to the moment it hits your teeth. So middlemen are eliminated, supplies and sales assured as far as they can be. Then there are economies of scale in buying supplies and equipment from outside. So far as the product is concerned, says Williams, 'While everyone else in Fast Food is processing rubbish, we are concentrating on being as natural as possible. We don't use frozen chips and we don't take the standardization of portions too far. The only modern concession is freezing the fish to keep it fresher.' In the training school over the Notting Hill premises, trainees are taught traditional, though standardized, techniques with traditional, though standardized, equipment.

Not many secrets here, then. If there is one, Williams believes it is in the management of staff, which is something the family shops must learn to cope with if they are coming into the High Street. London, with its volatile, shifting labour force, mainly of foreigners, is a manager's nightmare. Says Williams:

'Who would want to work seventy hours a week in a Fish & Chip shop! We used to have a complete staff turnover every three months; now 75 per cent of our women have been with us for over a year. We give them nice surroundings and try to make the company exciting to work for by getting its name in the papers and so on. But incentives are the key to it. Managers are paid a basic salary, *plus* bonuses geared to their performance on turnover, profit and wages. Some of the older men have never had a holiday, so there are holiday vouchers and trips to Paris, which makes the wives happy. For the serving staff there are Booster Weeks, with 1p. bonus for every portion of halibut (or whatever it is) sold. It all goes into a branch kitty, the Serve and Prosper Fund, which is shared out among them all. Then there's a loyalty bonus, four pence an hour after they've stayed with the firm three months. That's paid quarterly, so every quarter they get a big present, which they love.

'People say to me you've got to be profit-orientated. But I say the first thing you've got to be concerned about is the staff, in order to make any profits. Unless you keep *them* happy, you can't earn the money to keep the shareholders happy. It seems to me incredibly obvious and simple...'

It echoes what Wilfred Bush was saying, at Harry Ramsden's. But very little is obvious to the traditional frier, wondering whether to gamble on his customers remaining as conservative as he is—which will mean his own standard of living being ground thinner and thinner between the millstones of rising costs and price-resistance—or whether to diversify, or expand. If a chain means as little as two or three shops, then there are more small, local, family chains like the Duces' than most people realize. I should expect this trend to accelerate, with local groups coalescing into medium-size regional chains.

The North of England, and places like Oldham which not long ago was reputed to have four hundred Fish & Chip shops, will probably be the last stronghold of the traditional family frier, just as it was his birthplace. In such a stronghold he may very well last another twenty or thirty years. But in the fickle, affluent South I foresee the Trade splitting between the specialist chain shops and the more diversified quick food bar, somewhere between a Fish & Chip shop and a café, in which something lamentably close to a big fish finger will vie for custom with hamburgers, chicken and pies.

And with wine and beer beginning to trickle into the Fish & Chip shops, it would not surprise me to see (as we are already seeing in the Seafarer deal) the pubs trying to annex Fish & Chips. Perhaps we shall be taken back to those mid-Victorian days when a tavern might ring with the cry: 'I'll stand fish round, gentlemen!'

13. Paper Wrappings

ish & Chips have never really been accepted as a subject for well-bred literature. Friers themselves being, in general, men of few letters, I attribute this neglect to the middle-class origins of most writers. Their minds, I fear, have been prejudiced by the comic image of the trade; it has not succeeded in establishing the heroic reputation of mining, fishing or farming. Even haberdashery has fared better.

The search for Fish & Chip literature has been a hard one. I have written earlier of the paucity of even technical books on the subject. The bibliographies and bookshops offer works on fishing, fish curing,

Horizontal 'rumbler' with Robinsons' gas engine

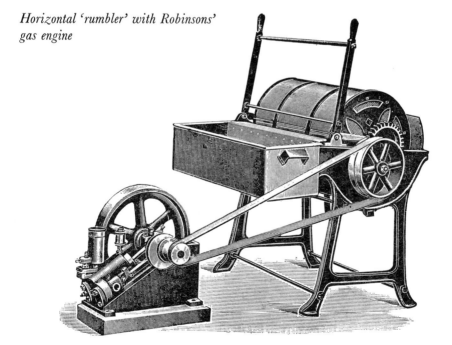

fish canning, fish sorting, fish farming and fish cooking, but nothing of an imaginative nature. With the exception of the examples culled from the Trade Press, most of the items in the following anthology have been stumbled on unexpectedly, and I am much obliged to my bibliophile friend George Engle for uncovering two of them.

My first example is, I am afraid, a little dishonest; for reasons which will appear at the end. I print it because I happen to be an addict of *lists*. (Cf. Spike Milligan's recording of a country auction catalogue, and Beachcomber's Directory of Huntingdonshire Cabmen).

On 8th November 1890, the columnist Bivalve noted in *The Fish Trades Gazette* that the Lord Mayor's Show was to be, that year, 'on a scale of extraordinary grandeur'. Bivalve submitted that it would not be out of *plaice* if the parade's *sole* aim were to illustrate the fish trade, and he proposed the following Order of March:

Police in fours
Band of the Billingsgate Market
Banner of Mr. Lawrence-Hamilton (with full list of degrees)
Car containing samples of bad smells, bacteria
microbes and other evils in bottles
Band of the Sanitas Works
Cod   Cod   Cod
Banner of the Fish Trades Gazette
Waggon drawn by Dromedaries containing specimens of
bled and gutted fish in peat moss
Band of The Devil's Own
The Billingsgate Ring (in invisible blue)
The Billingsgate Chaplain
Police
Costermongers
Large families in groups
Band of Shadwell Market
Police   Police
Banner of 'Bivalve'
Soles, Plaice, Turbot in boxes, baskets and heaps
Haddock-smokers of the Borough in uniform
Banner of 'Caudal Fin'
Detectives
Dragoon Guards
Royal Surrey Militia
The Brighton Mermaid
Banner of Ananias
Band of the Nore Sprat-catchers

Dried Sprats, Smoked Sprats, and Wet Sprats in boxes and barrels
LIFEBOAT IN CAR
Grimsby Fishing Smacks
Yarmouth Bloaters in boxes making a trophy twenty feet high
Banner of MacDonald
Band of the Whitstable Oyster Trade
Natives in Barrels
Natives in Bags
Natives on Foot
Detectives
Police two abreast
Triumphal Cars with allegorical representation of the
Newfoundland Fishery Difficulty
French Fisherman, two by two
Banner exhibiting the latest telegrams from Newfoundland
Banner of the Horse Marines
Banner of the Hon. Company of Whelk Peelers
The Worshipful Master of the Shrimpers
The Grand Master of the Penny Winkle Boilers
Grand Car showing the chief points of interest in the
Canadian Fishery Troubles
Group of Americans
Banner of McKinley
Members of the Worshipful Company of Oyster Openers
Cargo of Frozen Lamb from New Zealand
Dish of Fish Restaurant Prawns, mounted in Gold
Frozen Hares from Russia
Huge gilt bowl of Turtle Soup
THE LORD MAYOR
Wagon load of Whitebait
Waiters two and two collecting tips
Banners of the Sheriffs, ex-Lord Mayors, Aldermen and Judges
Police, soldiers and civilians
Cart of City Sewers

Apart from the intriguing 'in jokes' that obviously pepper the list (who, for example, was Mr. Lawrence-Hamilton, that he deserved this dig at his educational qualifications?) the really fascinating thing about it is that *there are no fish-friers in it at all.* Winkle-boilers, sprat-catchers and oyster-openers are admitted, and even costermongers. But the snobbery of the Billingsgate Press towards the friers is at its most impenetrable.

Forty years later, it had relented. For it was in *The Fish Trades Gazette*

(*and Poultry, Game and Rabbit Trades Journal,* to give it its full title) that
I found the only Fish & Chip novel that has come to my notice:

JOHNNY HIGGINBOTTOM AND HIS EXPERIENCES IN THE FISH TRADE
A Fried Fish Trade Yarn
Specially written in 14 Chapters

Inevitably the author was none other than William Loftas, Chatchip
at it again, and there are excellent grounds for believing that a large
part of it is autobiographical. Publication began on 30th May 1925.
What follows is my own synopsis.

Johnny Higginbottom is born in a little Yorkshire village, the son of a
farm foreman. Setting off to seek his fortune he takes a room in Sheffield,
luckily finding a godfearing landlady. He finds work delivering coal and
then as a builder's hod-carrier. He learns to smoke, but never drinks.

Every week Johnny puts a few shillings into the Post Office Savings
Bank. After a fall while hod-carrying, he gets new work as a carter at
the Fish Market, which brings him thirty shillings a week. His diligence
impresses his employer, and he is made manager of a fish shop, a post
he is to hold for the next three years.

'Johnny, like all the rest of the healthy young men of his time . . .
had done a bit of clean, harmless flirting and spooning with girls on
occasions . . .'

He meets Edna Turner, the daughter of a nearby grocer, while serving her four nice haddocks. 'She had a cheery and open countenance,
straight as an arrow as boarding-school girls usually are . . . She had
unaccented perfect English, marking her as a little superior to most of
the girls Johnny had hitherto met. Beyond that she was just an ordinary
English girl.'

They go for country walks together; but Edna's father does not
approve. 'The idea,' he said, 'of a fishmonger's assistant having the
cheek and impudence to aspire to the courtship of a respectable grocer's
daughter, and her with a boarding-school education and all . . . This
thing must be nipped in the bud and all future intercourse with this
young man must be stopped . . . If he'd been a grocer or even a butcher
one might have tolerated such an acquaintance. But a fishmonger!'

Edna is also being courted by Arthur, the son of Johnny's fishmonger
employer, which complicates matters for a chapter or two. But Arthur
is rejected by Edna, and with the approval of Edna's mother ('He has
grit, brains and adaptability') Johnny gets the girl. After all, he also has
'two or three hundred pounds in Consols and the Post Office Bank'. He
decides to invest the money in a business of his own, and finds it easier
to buy a fried fish shop than a wet one. It costs him £95 cash.

Queueing on the left: Harry Ramsden's after 1972 facelift

Battery frying for the masses: Ramsden's 1972 kitchen during a 'dry run'

Together, Johnny and Edna launch their little business, frying away side by side. He starts work at the not-too-onerous hour, one would have thought, of 8.30 a.m., peeling and washing for two-and-a-half hours with an old horizontal rumbler. Frying did not actually begin until half-past five in the evening, except on Fridays and Saturdays when they did a lunch-time session as well. They closed at eleven or half-past eleven at night.

Johnny has advanced religious views and little use for formal dogma: 'Love and fear God, love and do right to his fellow men, nothing else mattered.' However, this does not stand in the way of his election as town councillor and ultimately Mayor. His apotheosis comes in a triumphant confrontation with the Medical Officer of Health and Sanitary Inspector, whom he frustrates in their *fiendish plot to have fish-frying declared an Offensive Trade.*

Such, then, is the plot of one of the forgotten minor gems of our literature. I do not know who has the film, television or operatic rights, but surely it has possibilities for all three. Myself, I favour a musical comedy.

I have already mentioned, on an earlier page, Pierre Picton's *A Gourmet's Guide to Fish and Chips*, which begins with an excellent short essay on the history of the Trade (even if it does perpetuate the error that *Oliver Twist* was published in 1851). It does not, however, fall into the category of imaginative literature. Somewhat closer to that mark is Derek Cooper's *The Bad Food Guide*, with its satirical account of how 'the grand smell of frying and the clouds of smoke pouring out of the open door bear witness to the dexterity of the Ramsbottom family, father, son and grandson, in the gentle art of frying'. The Ramsbottoms could not possibly have been Federation members.

Elsewhere, the references are few and mainly farcical. There are, for example, two tiny poems in the Penguin *Yet More Comic and Curious Verse* of 1959; one of which, by A. G. Prys-Jones, speaks of a modern Helen who 'could have launched a thousand ships' feeding that face on 'fish and chips'; while the other, by G. C. Norman, speculates that Space-men will provision their 'unearthly trips' with 'atomic fission chips' ha-ha.

The Eleventh Pan Book of Horror Stories (1970) has a peculiarly horrible tale by Martin Waddell, 'Fried Man', which is set in the Valentia Supper Saloon and turns upon the (I am glad to say false) assumption that it is possible to stuff an entire dead body into one of the pans of a frying range. A badly conducted shop it is too, in all respects: with the frier failing to skim his chip pan before dumping in a new load. In literature, the Trade is mostly the victim of outsiders.

My next offering, however, purports to come from the inside. It is a unique example of a Fish & Chips Ghost Story, set in the Bucks-Northamptonshire border country, some fifty years ago:

Shark: alleged with Chips in Sydney

THE LOCK

Sam Jackson seemed to have been frying since birth. His shop, which had belonged to his parents before him, stood at one end of a small hump-backed bridge over a canal, beside one of the locks. As the barges moved up and down the canal, on their way between London and Birmingham, the bargees would ride ahead on their hard, iron bicycles to set the lock-gates for the oncoming boats and put in an order at the Fish Shop.

The lock served also as a footbridge between the shop and the Cage of Birds, a public house a little way off down the towpath. For one reason and another, there was a good deal of toing and froing across the lock beams.

Sam's wife, Mary, was twenty years younger than he, a girl out of the farmlands, sturdy and full of the promise of fruitfulness. But the promise was not fulfilled, and their disappointment with each other in this respect sickened and saddened their private moments. In public, however, they seemed a dutiful couple and Mary's hearty appearance and good humour ensured them a steady flow of loyal custom. The bachelor bargees, in particular, loitered and stared hungrily across the counter as Mary leant forward for a bucket of chips, or absent-mindedly wiped her hands over those noble haunches. There was one young bargee above all, Tom Stringer, with tawny hair, a chest like a keg of ale and hips so narrow they'ld slip through a pantry window, who would stop at nothing to ensure that his boats came past at frying-time. The very first time their eyes met, he and Mary could feel invisible arms groping for each other. Even so, they were lucky if the boats came past as often as once a fortnight.

One evening, by whipping his tow-horse a lot harder than usual, Tom managed to get his pair moored below the fish shop, and walked over the gate-beams to order 'tuppenny cod and penny chips three times', as supper for himself and his aunt and uncle (who made up the rest of the crew). As Sam, with his back to the counter, plunged a fresh basket of chips into the old, coal-fired wall range, Tom stooped over and whispered to Mary 'Will you be getting away this evening, my love?' He was a cheeky one, too.

Mary twitched the corner of her mouth, half-pleased, half-fearful, and nodded towards her husband. 'He'll be off for his drink, half-past nine,' she murmured, and then, loudly, *'Salt and vinegar on them all?'*

It had become Sam Jackson's habit to drown his marital sorrows in beer. So just before half-past nine he made the usual excuse that 'This shop is as hot and dry as Hell', adding 'I'll just pop across the lock to the Birds before it closes.' Mary, who knew better than to reproach him, lent positive encouragement on this occasion. It being a quiet country town, they normally shut the shop early on weekdays, and Mary offered to clean up while Sam took his drink in easy time.

No sooner had he heard the frier cross the lock than Tom was in at the back and his hand down Mary's bodice. There was no point wasting words or time, and they enjoyed each other vigorously in the potato store for more than twenty minutes. Then, pushing Tom away, Mary warned him the shop must be clean by the time her husband got back, or he would want to know where the lost hour had gone. Together they skimmed the pans, raked the ashes and swept the floor; and when Sam came lurching back over the lock gates, it was as if the Little People had done their good deed. Not that Sam noticed the difference.

Next day, the barges moved on before Sam had dragged himself down to the railway station to collect the day's fish. But Tom managed to prolong the affair by a second night, by bicycling down the towpath from his next halt, and back again. The deception continued in this way for almost half a year.

It was late in January when Mary realized she was no longer infertile. She had continued to do her wifely duty by Sam on the rare occasions that he was capable of demanding it, so there was no reason why the child should not, in principle, have been his. But she was certain that in practice it was not. The thought of that gross, beery Bag of Lard claiming her Tom's seed as his own was too much for her. And for Tom, too.

One bitter night as, by a coincidence, Tom's boats were tied up near the bridge once more, there was an accident. As Tom explained it to the police, he had been relieving himself on the towpath below the lock when he saw Sam Jackson scrambling drunkenly along the top of the gates, on his way back from the Cage of Birds. Tom had run to offer him a hand, but while he was still a dozen yards away the drunkard had slipped and fallen. Tom had plunged in to rescue him, but like most bargees he could not swim and the effort had done no good. The frier's body was found next morning at the lock downstream.

Nobody was much surprised when, still young and lusty and clearly in need of a helping hand, Mary was married to Tom at the end of summer. The baby was born on what should have been their honeymoon, if they had taken one; but they did not, seeing there was nobody to mind the business and they could afford no unpaying days after the cost of the funeral.

Tom managed somehow to master the rudiments of frying. But what with the baby squalling in the back room and the customers complaining of delays in the front, his temper grew shorter and shorter as the winter days drew in. The gipsy life he had led on the boats had made him a poor time-keeper, and he was careless with fire. Or that, at least, was the explanation accepted in the town for what followed.

One night, Tom awoke to a smell of burning. 'God damn you, Mary! Why didn't you rake the range out?' he roared. 'So help you, I did!' Mary retorted, 'Though it's the man's job, as everyone in the Trade knows but you.'

Tom hurried down the stairs and into the shop, to find the firebox full, the draught-port open and the range roaring like a March gale. He brought it under control and stormed back to bed for a ruined night of tears and argument.

They might have lived on no more unhappily than most, if that had been the last episode of its kind. But it was not. Several times the range stoked and kindled itself in the night, bringing the pans of fat near to flash-point and complaints of the smell from all the neighbours. Several times whole sacks of potatoes were strewn all over the floor of the shop. Several times there was coal in the bags of batter-flour. And on two dreadful occasions, dripping was smeared over the walls and floors of the fish shop. Tom and Mary had never heard the word 'poltergeist', but they had no doubt that the ghost of Sam Jackson was working out its revenge upon them.

On the last, most terrible night of all, the range was ablaze yet again and a strong wind was drawing the fire up the chimney. The stove-pipe at the back of the range was beginning to glow dull red as Tom burst in and seized the fire-irons to choke down the flames. But, to his fury, a new trick had been played. Something—a tray of fillets? a basket of chips?—had been tossed into the left-hand pan and the pan-cover pulled down over it. Whatever it was surged and hissed like a snake in Hell, and seemed to utter a small, pale cry.

Mary, who had paused to comfort the baby before following her husband down the stairs, could never be certain of her own eyewitness. So how can we tell what it was, exactly, that Tom saw as he opened the pan-cover and gazed in?

'It was all smoke and steam and flames in there. And when he opened that lid, he just stood staring into the burning fat. And then he cried out, "It's *you* in there—it's *you*—I'll get you out of there!" And then, you see,

Layout for the twenties: A. drains; B. peeler; C. motor; D. marble slab;
E. sink; F. chip bath; G. peel filter; H. motor switch; I. tap

he sort of dives in like he was going to pull a ferret out of a hole, and the
dripping flares out into his face, and there he is all red and swollen and
screaming with his hair on fire, and the first thing I know he's burst out
of the window and on to the bridge and off the bridge and into the
water. They say he'ld have died of shock anyway; but it was drowning,
too, like my first husband.'

Time for the lighter side of Fish & Chips literature. Verse if not
Poetry, has always been the people's literature. Being easier to remember
than prose, it needs no printing. Thus we have the Merseyside mocking-
song:

> Illy-willy apple-pips,
> Sally Taylor's got big hips,
> Saw her knickers full of rips,
> All the sailors of the ships
> Say that she's got greasy lips
> 'cos of eating Fish and Chips.

Perhaps a little less memorable is the ditty presented in the December
1970 edition of *The Fish Friers Review* by John Rouse (Oldham) Ltd.:

ODE TO A FRIER
or your leader is alive and well and
working in booth street

Frying can be trying

when your range is not
so good
so when you think of buying
please take care
John Rouse the top
trendsetter
gives you ranges that are
better
and a supersonic service
fair and square.

After one or two readings, it will be apparent that the form used is essentially traditional and that the absence of punctuation and capitals is deceptive. Either way, though, it is no Ode.

The most ambitious Fish & Chip poem is undoubtedly another 'Ode' —still lacking in the required rhythmic variety, but closer in the exaltation of its address—published in the August 1968 *Review*. From the scholarly echoes of Pope and Dryden in its heroic couplets, I suspect that although published anonymously its authorship is to be attributed to the editor himself:

ODE TO A NOBLE DISH
You Chinese connoisseurs with palates fine
May sing the joys of 'Number 29';
You vulgar rich with wallets gaping wide
May boast the savour of Kentucky Fried.
A nobler theme awaits my trembling lips:
The merits and the praise of *Fish And Chips*.
Theme nobler yet and of more serious vein
Than those which poets used to entertain,
Of antique chivalry in days of yore,
Of dragons, jousts, adultery and war.
Oh, who can sing in verse or otherwise
The glories of the frying enterprise?
Certain it is that I—of poets least—
Can't tell in rustic rhyme the royal feast,
Subject demanding Shakespeare's pen, not mine,
Whose simple couplets reach not the divine.
Yet, so that those in after times may cherish
Great Britain's great tradition (never perish!)
I set in clumsy phrase these faltering lines
Where those that love their chips may read the signs.
First to the preparation room we turn,
To look behind the scenes, the process learn:

Lo, where the honest frier daily stands
Wielding his steady knife with practised hands,
Poises his sharp blade and with canny thrust
Divides his fillets into portions just
As when a surgeon trusty lancet plies
And guides it through the flesh with eagle eyes
Or as the keen-brained justice wields the law
Between two parties, which should have the more,
Weighs equally by Act and Precedent
And gives to each reward or increment,
Thus does this frier cut his shilling pieces:
So many to the stone, and, all done, ceases.

Next does our frier broach without salute
His cellar, where the dark skinn'd Andean root
Lurks close in hempen sack or six-ply bags
All cleanly dressed and bearing tell-tale tags.
Taking from each a sample bright and fair,
He lugs them up and 'gins the chips prepare.
Next, grasping hard the sack upon his hips,
He heaves them up and into the peeler tips;
As when a railway tower reaches down from its height
Draws up a truck with majesty and might
Until the heavy waggon at the top
Spins on its side and lets its cargo drop
Into the hopper, with rumble and with roll,
While far below the engine gulps the coal,
Just hear the rumble as the peeler turns
Sloshing with muddy water as it churns.
Quickly extracting all his white-skinn'd prize,
The ruthless frier cuts out all their eyes.
On his remorseless face no pity's seen.
He throws them next into the chip machine,
There meets the root, midst whirling blades, its limit:
It's turned to chips at forty pounds a minute.
Now turns the frier to his seething pans,
And takes a portion in his spotless hands,
Twixt thumb and finger held with rapid swish
He bathes the morsel in the batter dish.
From dish to pan in one fell swoop it glides,
Kissing the fat as in its depths it hides.
As, when some liner through a channel wends
The watchful skipper o'er his compass bends,
So tends the frier his dials and his taps,

Not stooping to 'Maybe,' 'I guess,' 'Perhaps,'
But knowing absolutely and past doubt
The time is right to lift the portions out.

See, rise from the silken fat the golden fish,
Fresh bathed and glowing, hot as any dish;
As when the eagle high o'er the glossy sea
Mounting rebuffs the wind with joyous glee;
Or, like young Phaeton in his father's car
Who scorched the Earth up with his borrowed star!
What pen can catch the glory of this sight?
This scrumptious fish, a vision of delight?
Well-cooked and crisp, with joyful crackling hiss!
Taste and enjoy, with sighs of happy bliss!
Your natural heritage and right! The Chip!
Hot from the pan (just feel it burn your lip!)
And now my song is sadly at an end;
I must put down my pen and homeward bend.
But e'er I go, dear reader, grant my wish:
When hungry, that you'll ask for *Chips & Fish*.

It is not just the classical allusions and Virgilian similes that encourage the attribution to Brian Ashurst, B.A., but the fact that he is a known railway enthusiast as well.

Bread (or finger) slicer

There remains a number of more trivial verses, including the following inevitable assemblage of Fish Puns, presented as:

A FRIER'S EPITAPH
My HAKES are cured; this ROCK they PLAICEd
Below, my SOLE's above—
HAD DOCKed long since. sHAL I BUT face

God's EELongated love?
What SAITHE the prophet? No more sea,
To FILLET no more ships.
My COD hast Thou deserted me?
Have I had all my CHIPS?
Yet LINGer not, my PORTION's sweet;
I've hoed a virtuous ROE.
Better to RANGE the heavenly streets
Than FRY in Hell below.

FIVE FRIERS' LIMERICKS

A travelling frier named Phipps
Called at Heaven on one of his trips.
He quickly sold God
Six penn'orth of Cod,
And St. Peter—two penn'orth of chips.

A frier (whose name doesn't matter)
Went suddenly mad as a hatter:
He went for his knife
And cut up his wife
And sold her as scallops in batter.

A widow who fried at Dunbar
Had a bust much admired, near and far.
When she asked 'Shall I wrap 'em?'
They said 'Don't let that happen!
Leave 'em all hanging out as they are!'

A frier of Gidear Park
Served only Piranha and Shark.
The baths in the town
Soon had to close down,
And no-one went out after dark.

There was an old frier from Thanet,
The honestest man on this planet:
It was really a shock
To find that his Rock
Was genuine, piping-hot granite.

14. Chips by the Way—An aphoristic anthology

FISH AND FISCALITIS.

Little Boy: "Please, Mr. Whiting, I want a penn'orth of fried fish and taters, and please father says will you wrop it in a 'Protection' newspaper?"

1904 Fish Trades Gazette: *earliest known Fish & Chips joke, probably referring to papers offering free accident insurance to the bearer*

THE CLASSIC ERA

'The fried fish sellers live in some out-of-the-way alley, and not infrequently in garrets, for even among the poorest class there are great objections to their being fellow lodgers on account of the odour of the frying...'

Henry Mayhew, *London Labour and the London Poor,* 1861.

'It is a petty trade, but, nevertheless, it is a source of considerable nuisance in some neighbourhoods, the offensive smell of the oil boiling and the fish frying spreading often through the whole length of the street where the shop is situated . . .'

Dr. Ballard, 1876.

'The frying of fish has been a familiar source of annoyance and cause of frequent complaint in this country for more than half a century.'

Sir Shirley Murphy (M.O.H. to L.C.C.), 1906.

'Fish . . . The brain is nourished by it, the nerves are quietened, the mind grows stronger, the temper less irritable, and the whole being healthier and happier when fish is substituted for butcher's meat.'

Dr. Mortimer Granville, 1881.

'For sale: Fish Supper Bar. Alamode potatoes and Stewed Eel business; thickly populated neighbourhood; proprietor having met with serious accident, cause of leaving. 10 Bedford Street, Commercial Road.'

Advertisement in *The Fish Trades Gazette*, September 1883.

'A great many fishfriers adulterate the vinegar. This does a very great deal of harm . . .'

The Fish Trades Gazette, 1904.

'How any human beings can stand the wear and tear of such a life is beyond my understanding.'

'A Lady Journalist' in *Pearson's Magazine*, 1905.

'I do not think there is a worse paid trade in the United Kingdom than ours, considering the hours we work, some of us from 6 in the morning till 11.30 at night.'

C. H. Benfield (Leciester Frier), 1907.

'Probably in the whole history of trades there is none which had so humble and unpleasant a beginning as the fried fish trade.'

Chatchip, 1909.

'The less there is in a fried fish shop the better.'   Chatchip, 1910.

'It is true to say the fried fish trade has done more in the cause of sobriety among our working people than all the temperance agencies combined.'

Chatchip, 1910

'In the First World War in France they were like ice-cream barrows . . . they used to stand on the Grand Place, specially at Lille . . . "Pom-di-terr frips" or something like that.'

Joe Lees of Mossley.

'A great industry and one of our country's assets.'

First issue *The National Fish Caterers Review*, 1925.

'Where is a youth more sure of finding a good practical mate than in the throngs of girls who patronize the fish restaurant, girls who are not too proud to take home a parcel of fish and chips?'

'Reformer', *The Fish Trades Gazette*, 1930.

MODERN TIMES

'Fish and Chips are part of the fabric of British Society.'

A. G. Williams of Associated Fisheries, 1971.

'I believe that batter is the one and only cause of black specks.'

Letter in *The Fish Friers Review*, 1948.

'It is time the trade throughout the country forgot for ever penny-worths—and twopenny portions, too.'

The Fish Friers Review, 1950.

'It used to be only fish and chips; today the fish and chip shop is becoming a cook shop . . .'

Fred Lewis of Wales, 1970.

'Alas poor Yorrick, thy pungent smell will waft no more . . . Perhaps Will Shakespeare could have phrased a better tribute to the closing of one of Stratford's most important buildings, the Ely Street fish and chip shop.'

The Fish Friers Review, 1970.

'A short while ago I went to a pisces and pomme de terre boutique . . .'

E. A. King, *The Fish Trades Gazette*, 1971.

'Fish and Chips are Trendy, Where It's At, Now—like Frank Zappa, Princess Anne, Dougal and Zebedee . . .'

Honey Magazine, 1970.

'Psychiatrists have said that eating fish and chips releases inhibitions.

It is the only food you can eat how, when and where you want it!'
The Fish Friers Review, 1970.

'You can eat them in the dark, and when you bite your fingers you know you've finished.'

B. H. Baldwin of High Wycombe.

'We consider ourselves the Rolls Royce of frying ranges.'

Representative of Acme Engineering.

'In spite of our name, we consider ourselves the Rolls Royce of frying ranges.'

Representative of Frank Ford Restaurant Engineers.

'Chester offers advice to chipper makers—"Eject Your Chips Vertically!"'

The Fish Friers Review headline, 1970.

'Is your fish browned off with an inferior batter?'

Advertisement for Crispex.

'Q: What gets paler the further North you go?
A: Batter.'

Old fishfriers' joke.

'It's child's play frying fish now.'

Leeds rangemakers' foreman, 1971.

'It's a particularly gruelling form of existence.'

Wilfred Bush, Manager of 'Harry Ramsden's', 1971.

'If we're going to have Fish and Chips—let's get it right!'

Wilfred Bush.

'See this microwave oven flash through your chicken, faggots, pies, puddings, peas, etc., at a shattering re-heat speed you never thought possible, making fast extra profits in a way no other equipment can.'

Advertisement in *The Fish Friers Review*, 1971.

'Dogfish have been feeling the pinch.'

Ministry of Agriculture & Fisheries, 1971.

'Chinese snacks, though good value and a pleasant change, do not replace Fish & Chips—as any Chinese proprietor of a fried fish shop will acknowledge.'

Editorial, *The Fish Friers Review*, 1971.

'After having seen them made at a well-known firm's premises and noting the type and quality of fish going into the huge mixing hoppers, I have never had another fish cake in my shop, nor have I eaten one.'

'Commoner' in *The Fish Friers Review*, 1971.

'Go to a caff for a meal—open the door and the helpings'll blow away.'

Albert Malin of Old Ford.

'Q: Where do American chip fanciers get their malt vinegar?
A: From Britain, and to be more exact from the Penistone Pure Malt Vinegar Co., who are at the moment flooding the U.S. market with their tart liquid . . .'

Advertisement in *The Fish Friers Review*, 1971.

'Fish 'n Chips, as a proletarian finger food, emerged from the humble Cockney-powered push-cart of the early nineteenth century into the brightly lit take-out emporia of the Gay 90s . . . Its traditional take-out packaging was newsprint—preponderantly, sheets torn from Britain's multi-million-circulation Sunday scandal sheet, *The News of the World*. Despite these lowly origins, Fish 'n Chips rapidly ascended the social ladder . . .'

Gallup Poll report (U.S.A.), 1971.

'Americans are not fish-orientated . . . The American public likes more batter than fish.'

Denis Malin of Old Ford, 1971.

'National Federation of Fish Friers' ties make a distinctive and attractive addition to any man's wardrobe . . .'

The Fish Friers Review, 1971.

'The National Federation of Fish Friers' is now able to offer members a 13 day Mediterranean cruise in December . . .'

The Fish Friers Review, 1971.

'Roughly 6,000 visitors thronged the Doncaster frying trades exhibition. The competition to find Miss Hot Chips in Hot Pants attracted forty-two entrants, including one female impersonator called Barry.'

The Fish Friers Review, 1971.

'Squid and Chips are now being sold in Edinburgh, mostly to those who acquired a taste for it while on holiday abroad.'

The Fish Friers Review, 1971.

'A new product which combines the best features of the popular fish finger with the delights of scampi has been launched . . . It is a prawn finger.'

The Fish Friers Review, 1971.

The Guardian, May 1972.

The Minister of State, Treasury, Mr John Nott fore-cast that the debate "will become enshrined in the annals of Parliament and be known as the fish and chip debate. It is the case that, if fish and chips are consumed on the premises, then they are liable to VAT but if they are taken away they are not liable to VAT."

'AFRICA MAY PROVIDE WORLD FISH AND CHIPS.'

Sunday Post (Nairobi), 5th December 1971.

'Only a Campbell would eat chips with Haggis.'

Miss Joan MacDonald.

'I don't mind getting Fish & Chips from an Italian or even a Greek; but it seems unnatural to get them from a Pakistani.'

Customer in Notting Hill.

'It is very embarrassing for a Hindu in Yorkshire—they *will* fry their fish in cow fat.'

Indian leaving fish shop in Leeds

'Chinese friers in Bristol are to be left to their own devices . . . for the time being at least.'

The Fish Friers Review, 1971.

'In 1961, Attercliffe, Sheffield, used to sell the best Fish and Chips in the World.'

Miss Jacky Gillott.

'You've never heard chips sing till you've heard them come out of the pan in the Rhondda.'

A Mr. Rees.

'If one requires fish and chips par excellence, the best place to get them is in a fish and chip café, eaten fresh from the pan. And I say this in spite of all the nonsense one hears that "they are best when eaten out of doors and from the paper wrappings". What a load of rubbish . . . Sacre bleu!'

'Commoner' in *The Fish Friers Review*, 1971.

 inis

Index

Illustrations in the text are indicated by *italic* numerals, and Plates by **bold**.

163

Index